W9-BIR-525

I think I need a
Lawyer,
Now What?!™

by Marci Alboher Nusbaum

SILVER
LINING
BOOKS

NEW YORK

Copyright © 2002 by Silver Lining Books
ISBN 0760726531

All rights reserved. No part of this book may be reproduced or
transmitted in any form or by any electronic or mechanical
means, including information storage and retrieval systems,
without permission in writing, with the exception of brief
passages used in a critical article or review.

First Edition
Printed and bound in the United States of America

This book is an overview of basic legal concepts, not a substitute for a lawyer or an
answer to every possible legal question. The aim of this book is to get the reader
acquainted with basic legal concepts so that the reader will be more informed when
speaking with a lawyer.

The laws touched upon in this book vary considerably from state to state and change
frequently. Be sure to consult a lawyer knowledgeable about the current laws in your
state if you have a particular legal problem. Note that the anecdotes and First Person
Disasters included in the book are hypotheticals created to illustrate particular
points rather than depictions of actual scenarios involving real people; any resem-
blance to actual persons is unintentional.

While Silver Lining Books and the author have used best efforts in writing this book,
they make no representations or warranties as to its accuracy and completeness.
They also do not make any implied warranties of merchantability or fitness for a particular purpose. Any advice given in this book is not guaranteed or warranted and it
may not be suitable for every factual situation. Neither Silver Lining Books nor the
author shall be liable for any losses suffered by any reader of this book.

For information, contact:
Silver Lining Books
122 Fifth Avenue
New York, NY 10011
212-633-4000

Other titles in the Now What?!™ series:
I'm turning on my PC, Now What?!
I'm turning on my iMac, Now What?!
I'm in the Wine Store, Now What?!
I'm in the Kitchen, Now What?!
I need to get in Shape, Now What?!
I need a Job, Now What?!
I haven't saved a Dime, Now What?!
I'm on the Internet, Now What?!
I just bought a Digital Camera, Now What?!
I'm Retiring, Now What?!
I'm getting Married, Now What?!
I've got a Grill, Now What?!
I need to give a Presentation, Now What?!
I want Cosmetic Surgery, Now What?!

Titles in the Now What?!™mini series:
I just got a Handheld Organizer, Now What?!
I just got a Cell Phone, Now What?!

introduction

Not only did her new car break down for the third time in a month, but now Gwen's homeowners' association was fining her for parking it on her own lawn. She was parking on the lawn because the contractor who was supposed to retar her driveway hadn't come back the next day to finish the job, even though she had paid him in full. "It's enough to make you scream. I am pretty sure I need a lawyer for at least one of these problems, but how do I know for sure? And what exactly will a lawyer do for me anyway?"

It was exactly these kinds of questions that led to the creation of **I think I need a Lawyer, Now What?!** It's an easy-to-understand guide that explains numerous aspects of the law that affect your life. So whether your problem is a faulty new car (lemon law, see page 90) or a breach of contract with your contractor (see page 46), the first line of defense is here. Along the way, you'll learn the meaning of many legal terms, how the law looks at some of life's everyday problems, and whether you need a lawyer to help solve them.

Barb Chintz
Editorial Director, the *Now What?!*™ series

table of contents

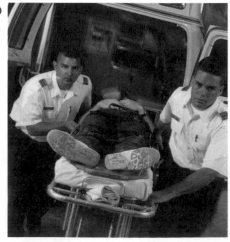

On the Job

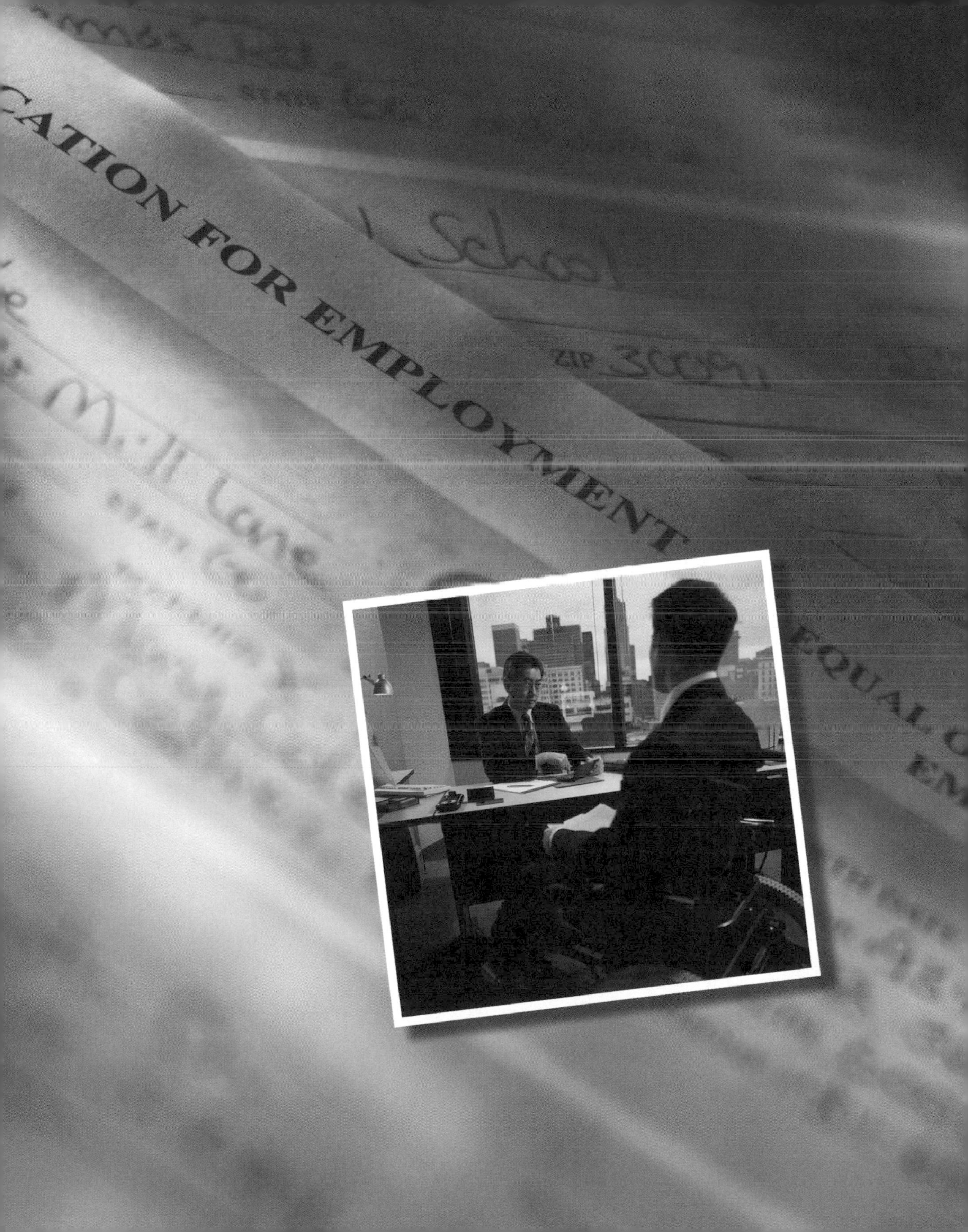
CATION FOR EMPLOYMENT

what is employment law?

When do you need a lawyer?

You get home from an interview and suddenly start wondering whether it was right that the interviewer asked you about your plans to raise a family. Or perhaps you've been working at a company for some time and someone you believe is less qualified than you has just been promoted above you. Maybe your boss has been taunting you with remarks you think are inappropriate for the workplace. If you find yourself with questions about your rights at work, it may be time to learn more about the laws that regulate employment. Or it may be time to meet with a lawyer who specializes in employment law (also called labor law).

Employers have a lot of leeway to hire, promote, and fire employees—but the employment relationship is not completely one-sided. As an employee (or even a job candidate), you have rights, too. There are many laws that protect the rights of employees, including wage and hour laws, antidiscrimination laws, laws regulating safety and other workplace conditions, and even laws protecting your privacy in the workplace.

Most people go through their entire career without ever consulting or hiring an employment lawyer. But if you have a problem your human resources department cannot resolve, you may need one.

How to Find an Employment Lawyer

Once you've decided you need an employment lawyer, how do you go about finding one? Talk to people you know who recently left a job or had a problem at work, and ask if they used a lawyer they would recommend. If you are concerned about age, gender, or race discrimination, civil rights organizations like the **American Civil Liberties Union** (**ACLU**) are helpful resources. Referrals are available at your local bar association or in legal directories like Martindale Hubbell (available at some libraries and on the Internet at **www.martindale.com**), **www.findlaw.com**, and the National Employment Lawyers Association (**www.nela.org**).

Questions for an Employment Lawyer

Have you handled this type of case before?

Employment law changes rapidly. Variations in state law can drastically affect your legal rights and how you can enforce them. It is important that the lawyer you hire has experience in the situation you face and is knowledgeable about the current state of the law.

How do you charge?

Many lawyers will take cases on a **contingency** basis, meaning you only pay if you win, and the fee comes out of the award you recover—often 30% to 40% of the total. If you are hiring a lawyer for a specific transaction like negotiating an employment or severance agreement, you need to find out what the lawyer charges.

Can you give me a realistic estimate of how long it will take to resolve the case?

Most lawyers should be able to give you a ballpark estimate of how long a case will take.

Are you available to take calls after hours?

When your case involves a problem at work, you may be uncomfortable handling calls with your lawyer from the office. You need to know if and when the lawyer can be contacted after business hours.

interviewing

What are your rights?

Employment law also covers your rights when trying to get a job. For instance, there are certain types of interview questions that are considered off-limits for employers questioning job candidates. Generally, these include questions about your marital status, age, religion, sexual orientation, race, citizenship, medical history, and whether you have physical or mental disabilities.

If you are asked a question about any of these topics, you have a right not to answer and your failure to answer should not affect your chance of getting the job. In fact, in some instances you might have a case against a potential employer if you believe that your answers or failure to answer such questions resulted in your not being selected for a job.

On the flip side, employers have wide leeway to question you about things that are relevant to your ability to do the job. For example, employers can ask you about your job experience and can contact references you provide. They can obtain information about your credit history if it is relevant to the job you are seeking, as long as you give your permission. And they can also ask you to submit to certain tests as part of the interview process. These tests may range from a simple personality quiz to a test on information necessary to do the job.

Reference Name: _____
Reference Title: _____
Reference Company: _____
Reference Phone: _____

Candidate's Name: _____
Position Applied For: _____
Date: _____
Completed By: _____

1. What was/is your professional relationship to him/her and over what time period did you work together?

2. What was his/her title, basic duties/responsibilities?

3. What are his/her most pronounced strengths?

4. What are his/her most pronounced areas in which improvement is necessary?

5. Can you tell me about a project/idea he/she initiated which made a positive impact on the organization?

6. Overall, what were/are your perceptions of his/her performance?

7. How would you describe his/her interpersonal and communication skills?

ASK THE EXPERTS

I have a slight physical disability. Is there anything I should know to protect my rights during an interview?

The Americans with Disabilities Act (commonly referred to as the ADA) is a federal law that protects employees against discrimination in the workplace. Under the ADA, employers are required to make reasonable accommodations for workers to do their jobs—and that protection extends to job applicants as well. So if you need certain accommodations during the interview process—for example, if you are deaf and require an interpreter for a certain test—you should feel comfortable making those needs known to your interviewer. You should also be aware that under the ADA, an employer cannot ask you about your disability unless it is for purposes of making an accommodation (e.g., whether you need a handicapped parking space). If you do ask for an accommodation, the employer is permitted to ask you for medical certification of the need as well as certification that you will be able to do the job you are seeking with the accommodation you request.

Keep in mind that the ADA only applies to employers with more than 15 people. One of the reasons for this is that larger companies have a greater ability to modify working conditions than small ones. Even among companies that are covered by the ADA, those with greater resources will be held to a higher standard for what is considered a reasonable accommodation.

After a first interview, I was asked to take a drug test. Do I have to?

Probably—if you want the job. Most states allow employers to require new employees to submit to a drug or alcohol test before beginning work, as long as they are seeking to ferret out illegal drug use. Drug testing of employees who are already hired is a different matter and such testing is often prohibited by law unless there are particular reasons to ensure that employees are not using drugs (e.g., truck drivers or others whose drug use could prove harmful to others).

11

working

Good news. You do have a basic legal safety net that covers your rights as a worker. This net was established by the federal government. For example, the most basic employment law sets the minimum wage, restricts child labor, and establishes a standard 40-hour workweek for many employees. It's called the Fair Labor Standards Act (FLSA). The FLSA protects the rights of men and women to receive equal pay for equal work. It also covers overtime pay. Under the Fair Labor Standards Act, employees who work on an hourly basis (also called **nonexempt** employees) are entitled to overtime pay if they work in excess of 40 hours in a workweek. Overtime pay is generally calculated at an hourly rate equal to one and a half times your normal rate of pay, but it varies for different jobs. If you believe your employer is paying you a salary and not by the hour to avoid paying you overtime, you should consult a lawyer (see page 9).

Privacy in the office

How much privacy do you have when using the telephone or e-mail at work? Perhaps not as much as you may think. This is because your employer owns the equipment you are using and that's why, in most circumstances, your company is allowed to access any material stored in that equipment. Even if you use a password, most employers can gain access to stored data—in some cases, even material the user has "deleted" (which has often been copied onto a backup system).

These days, employers routinely monitor Web sites visited by their employees. Abuse of office e-mail or Internet access (for example, by visiting inappropriate sites or clogging the server with lengthy downloads) is a good way to get yourself into serious trouble at work.

Monitoring of telephone calls is less common, although many states allow employers to monitor telephone calls if employees have been notified and consented in advance to the monitoring. Voice mail is another matter. Courts are still looking into whether employees have an expectation of privacy in their office voice mail.

ASK THE EXPERTS

My first day on the job, I was asked to sign a confidentiality agreement. Should I?

A **confidentiality agreement** is a document in which you promise not to reveal any proprietary or other confidential information that you acquired on the job. Employers use these agreements to protect their client base and business practices from being raided. In companies that are particularly cautious about their proprietary data, everyone from mail clerk to senior vice president will be asked to sign one. These agreements are enforceable—meaning you can be sued if you breach them.

What if my company asks me to sign a noncompete agreement?

A **noncompete agreement** restricts the employee's rights to accept certain types of employment after his employment with the current employer ends. Say you accept a job as marketing director for a software company—you may be asked to sign a noncompete agreement not to work for another software company for a certain period of time after you cease working for your current employer. Such agreements are not always enforceable (in fact, they are illegal in some states). Where they are enforceable, they must be reasonable both in terms of length of time and geographic scope. For example, a company can't restrict you from working in the software industry anywhere in the United States for the rest of your life. If you have any doubts about the reasonableness of what the company is asking, talk to a lawyer before signing.

How can I find out if I am being paid properly for my job?

If you have a question about whether you are being properly paid for the time you work, you can contact the federal Department of Labor's Wage and Hour Division (Room S302, 200 Constitution Avenue, NW, Washington, DC 20210; 202-219-8305).

health and safety

What your employer legally has to provide

Some might say the very idea of working is unhealthy. But given that most of us need a paycheck, you should know what is expected of your employer when it comes to matters of health and safety. Although employers are not required to offer health insurance for their employees, they are generally required to provide **disability insurance** (which provides employees with income for the amount of time they cannot work due to an injury or illness).

The responsibility varies by state and by the size of the company, but you can expect to receive some benefits if you can't do your job after becoming disabled. If you are severely disabled, you may also qualify for Social Security disability benefits.

You also have a right to expect that your job won't expose you to known health risks. Under the Occupational Safety and Health Act (OSHA) and various state laws, employers must protect employees from known hazards, ensure that buildings comply with safety standards, create plans for emergency evacuations, and provide warnings about dangerous substances in the workplace.

If you feel that there is a safety hazard in your workplace, inform your supervisor. If no action is taken, you can file a complaint under OSHA. Most states protect employees who blow the whistle on their employer's misconduct and prohibit retaliation against an employee who lodges a complaint. For more detailed information about workplace safety, or to report a potential violation, contact the Occupational Safety and Health Administration, 200 Constitution Avenue, NW, Washington, DC 20210, 202-219-7162 (**www.osha.gov**).

ASK THE EXPERTS

I want to leave my job but am nervous about my health insurance because I have a preexisting health condition. What should I do?

Under a federal law called the Health Insurance Portability and Accountability Act of 1996 (HIPAA), employees covered under an employer's group medical plan are allowed to carry their insurance from one employer to the next in many situations. This law was enacted to avoid the problem employees faced when preexisting medical conditions prevented them from changing jobs because a new employer's plan would exclude them. Your employer should be able to supply you with the necessary forms to take care of this.

I'm having some personal problems and would like to see a therapist under my company's health plan. Will my boss find out about this?

The highest level of privacy afforded an employee is reserved for medical records. For that reason, many employers have their medical benefits administered through their healthcare provider. If they do need to see the information, they're required to maintain it in a confidential manner and not release information to anyone in the workplace except those who need to know—for example, your company's plan administrator.

workers' compensation

If you're hurt on the job

Employers are also required to carry **workers' compensation insurance**. This insurance compensates employees for medical expenses from injuries sustained on the job. Workers' compensation can also include reimbursement for lost wages if you missed work because of your injury, and rehabilitation costs, such as physical therapy. The amount you could receive varies by state, but don't expect your costs to be covered completely. You can generally expect to receive half to two-thirds of your expenses—and there will likely be a cap on the total amount you can receive. Workers' compensation can also provide temporary or permanent disability coverage if your injury prevents you from returning to work.

Injuries covered by workers' compensation include obvious cases (e.g., you hurt yourself when a piece of machinery malfunctions) and also some less obvious ones (e.g., you fall and break your leg at the off-site holiday party). Coverage can also extend to business travel, long-term repetitive injuries, and other situations where you can establish that the injury was caused by some activity you were engaged in because of your job.

But workers' compensation doesn't cover every worker or every type of job, so you'll need to check with your lawyer to see whether you're eligible. If you work for a small company, are an independent contractor, or work in someone's home or on a farm, you may not be covered.

ASK THE EXPERTS

I've developed carpal tunnel syndrome from the typing I do at my job. Is that the type of injury that would be covered by workers' compensation insurance?

It may be. When you go to your doctor, your physician will determine whether he believes the injury is job-related. If he decides that it is, he will send his bill directly to your employer. If he determines that it is not employment-related but that the injury prevents you from working, you may still qualify for disability benefits. There are deadlines for filing a claim for workers' compensation, which vary by state; be sure to immediately report your injury to your employer.

I work for a company that is not covered by the workers' compensation laws in my state. Do I have any options to get reimbursed for expenses I incurred from an on-the-job injury?

You might, depending on the situation involved in your injury. But you will likely have to hire a lawyer and file a lawsuit against your employer. See pages 96–108 for a discussion of personal-injury lawsuits.

I got into a fight while on the job and have suffered many injuries. Can I submit my bills to my employer?

You can, but depending on the facts of the situation, it is unlikely that your injuries will be covered by your employer. Employers are generally not held financially responsible for injuries to their employees when the conduct that caused the injury was illegal or violated company rules. So if fights are prohibited on the job site and you started the fight, you're probably on your own when it comes to your medical bills.

taking a leave of absence

When you need to take time off

What if you want to take time off for the arrival of a new baby or to care for a family member who is ill? Because of a federal law called the Family Medical Leave Act (FMLA), you may be entitled to take up to three months off without fear of losing your job.

Of course, there are some catches—notable among them is that this law only applies to employers with 50 or more employees and there is no requirement that your employer has to pay you during your time off. But if you take advantage of the FMLA, your healthcare and other benefits must continue during your leave, and your employer will be required to hold your job for you until you return. Employers subject to the FMLA are also required to post an explanation of the law's benefits in the workplace.

Another area where you can expect to be allowed unpaid time off is when you are required to meet your civic responsibilities. If you need to take time off to serve on a jury or vote, your employer must hold your job for you until you return. If you need to take time off to perform military service and your service lasts 5 years or less, your employer must offer you a similar position upon your return.

ASK THE EXPERTS

How many vacation days am I entitled to by law?

Sorry to break it to you, but no law requires an employer to provide you with a set amount of vacation time. Policies on vacation and sick days vary by company and are among the benefits packages that companies put together to attract talented employees.

I'm in the Army Reserve, and I think I'm going to be called up for active duty. Will my job be waiting for me when I finish serving?

It should be. Various state and federal laws make it unlawful for an employer to discriminate in employment or reemployment on the basis of military service, and these laws protect the jobs of those who need to take leave for military duty. Those same laws also impose requirements on the employee to notify the employer in advance of the leave and promptly upon return. Your rights would vary based upon the length of time you are away from the workplace.

Must I tell a prospective employer that I'm four months pregnant?

So long as you can perform all the the essential functions of the position for which you applied, you are not obligated to disclose your condition. Importantly, employers are prohibited by federal antidiscrimination laws from asking you during the application and interview process if you are pregnant or plan to be in the future.

discrimination and sexual harassment

Fighting illegal work practices

One of the most important rights you have in the workplace is the freedom from discrimination. Discrimination occurs when an employee suffers unfair treatment based on some characteristic that is unrelated to performance. Among the characteristics protected by law are age, race, gender, religion, sexual orientation, physical or mental disability, and marital status. (However, some discrimination laws only apply to employers with a certain number of employees, and the laws can vary by state.)

Age-based discrimination is an area that has gotten a lot of attention in recent years. The federal Age Discrimination in Employment Act (ADEA) provides protection to workers 40 and over by making it illegal for companies to eliminate older workers (high-income earners who often have more benefits based on seniority).

Another form of discrimination often in the news is sexual harassment, which can take two forms. The first is the classic "if you go out with me, I'll get you a raise" scenario. The second type, known as **hostile work environment**, occurs when unwelcomed sexual advances, requests for sexual favors, and other verbal or physical conduct of a sexual nature are so severe or pervasive as to alter the conditions of an employee's job. In other words, the employee feels uncomfortable going to work.

While the former is easy to spot, the latter is not. Behavior such as spreading rumors about a person's sex life, repeatedly asking someone out who is not interested, and displaying calendars with images of nude men or women have all been found by courts to establish or contribute to a claim of hostile work environment.

Following corporate policy

Most large companies have a policy about dealing with harassment and discrimination. If you do have a complaint, go to your human resources department and report it. They should investigate the complaint and take appropriate disciplinary action. If you still aren't satisfied, then consider contacting a lawyer.

My boss has been taunting me with lewd comments lately. What can I do?

Check with your human resources department and find out if your company has a policy for handling sexual harassment complaints. If so, follow the procedures it sets forth and see if the company remedies the problem. If it doesn't, you may want to report the behavior to the Equal Employment Opportunity Commission (EEOC) or your state's fair-employment agency. Keep in mind that employers are prohibited from demoting, firing, or otherwise penalizing you for filing such a complaint—and you would be able to bring a suit against your employer for any retaliation that occurred. You can also talk to a lawyer to see if you have a case worth pursuing.

No woman has ever been promoted from my position, and I know that many who have held the job before me were qualified. Would this constitute discrimination?

It may violate not only the sexual discrimination laws but also the federal Equal Pay Act—if the company has a tradition of paying women less money than it pays similarly qualified men. These are hard cases to prove, but if you feel there has been an injustice, you should consult a lawyer to see if it would be worthwhile to bring a claim or lawsuit.

How far does my employer have to go to accommodate my disability?

Under the Americans with Disabilities Act (ADA), the federal law that protects against discrimination based on physical or mental disabilities, employers are required to provide an employee who can perform the essential functions of the job with "reasonable accommodations." What is reasonable will depend on the size of the company and the disability. As a practical matter, the greater a company's resources the more it will be expected to do in order to accommodate a disabled worker. Keep in mind that only employers with 15 or more employees are subject to the ADA—and that not every condition qualifies as a disability under the law.

leaving your job

Go out in style

You've gotten a new job. Or perhaps you have just had it with your old job and want out now. How exactly do you tell your current employer that you're leaving? If you want to ensure that nothing from your departure comes back to haunt you, you should resign in a way that doesn't burn any bridges or subject you to any legal liabilities. A few things to keep in mind:

- Give your employer fair notice so that you don't leave people with a mess to clean up. (There is no legal requirement, but some employers require two weeks—an amount of time generally deemed to be reasonable.)

- If you have an employment contract or any other document that outlines the terms of your employment, review it to make sure that you understand any restrictions on your postemployment activities.

- Return any property belonging to your employer.

- If you are resigning by letter, keep it brief. And if there is any chance you'll want to sue your employer, have a lawyer review the letter.

- Avoid bad-mouthing your employer. You never know, you just may find yourself working with former colleagues again.

- Do not remove property or confidential information that you know belongs to the company.

I'm leaving my job. Could I get in trouble if I take copies of work I produced, so I can use them at my new job?

This is a very touchy area. Most of what you produce on the job ultimately belongs to your employer, not to you. This is particularly true if you signed a **work-for-hire** agreement, which states that you do not retain any rights in creative work that you produce. Work that you create may also be considered a **trade secret** (like a chemical formula or business plan), and you could get into trouble by taking such data with you. Even so, you may be entitled to take samples of your work for your portfolio. In order to protect yourself, talk about this with your boss or someone in human resources.

FIRST PERSON DISASTER STORY

The pen is mightier than the mouth

When I announced to my boss that I had gotten a job with another firm, she was really upset. She begged me to stay on and offered me a really nice raise, effective immediately. I decided to stay and turned down the job offer. Three months went by and I still hadn't seen any evidence of my raise. When I talked to my boss about it, she said it was coming, but there was just some red tape. Six months later my raise came through, but it was not retroactive. I was furious. Turns out there was nothing I could do about it. Later, a lawyer friend of mine told me to always get offers in writing. —Katherine S.

being let go

**What to know
before you go**

Unless you are a very senior-level employee or you sign an agreement for a term of employment, most jobs are considered **employment at will**—which means that you can be fired at any time. But you still have some rights regarding how and why you are fired.

Termination without cause—If you are terminated without cause, that generally means the loss of your job is not related to your conduct. Layoffs or downsizings, where your termination is part of a program in which a number of employees are let go, fall into this category. If your termination is without cause, you will likely be eligible to collect unemployment insurance as well as any specific benefits your company makes available, like **severance** (the continuation of full or partial salary and/or benefits for a certain period of time) or **outplacement services** (assistance in finding a new job).

Termination for cause—This means you were terminated for some misconduct or behavior on the job and you will likely not be eligible for unemployment insurance or any other benefits your company offers to those terminated without cause.

Resignation—Here you decide to leave, or the company has made the decision to let you go but allowed you to say you resigned so that you have a better story to tell the outside world. If you resign, you will generally not be eligible for unemployment insurance or company benefits. So if you are offered the option of resignation or termination, make sure you understand exactly what benefits you will receive in either scenario.

I've been fired from my job. Is my employer required to give me severance?

Employers are not legally required to provide severance payments, but many employers do so. If your employer doesn't have such a program, consider asking for some type of severance. One incentive for employers to offer severance is that their former employees will be less inclined to sue them.

My employer has asked me to sign a release in order to obtain a better severance package. Should I sign?

A **release** is basically a promise not to sue. In some cases you're entitled to certain benefits whether or not you sign a release—so before you sign any agreement make sure you are not giving up any basic right (e.g., the right to work for a competitor) without obtaining something valuable in return like severance payments, additional compensation, or outplacement services. This is an important decision, and you should take some time before making it. In fact, there are some laws that require employees be given specific periods of time to consider signing a release—and if you are 40 or over or were part of a downsizing, you may be eligible for the waiting period.

Unemployment insurance

If you lose your job, you may be eligible to receive unemployment insurance payments until you get back on your feet. The amount of money you can collect varies, but the payments will replace some percentage of your prior income and can continue for up to 6 months. Coverage is typically limited to those who lose a job through no fault of their own (some resignations fall into this category). It is best to apply for unemployment insurance soon after you lose your job, because it often takes several weeks for the payments to begin.

To apply, you will need to call or go in person to your local unemployment office, depending on your state's process. Be sure to have proof of your identity (a driver's license or passport will do) as well as proof of your loss of employment—for example, a termination letter from your employer or your last pay stub. Once you begin receiving payments, you will have to contact the unemployment office periodically and state that although you're seeking employment, you remain unemployed. In some states, you can do this online or by telephone.

now what do I do?
Answers to common questions

Can my employer search my office?

The legality of a workplace search is analyzed by balancing the employee's expectation of privacy with the employer's need to perform an investigation. If you're given a locked drawer, for example, you would probably expect that your boss won't be poking around in that drawer. But if your company has notified all employees that management retains the right to access areas where personal belongings are kept, you should lower your expectations. In instances where improper conduct, criminal behavior, or impending danger exists, your employer would probably be justified in searching even those areas where you might normally have a high expectation of privacy.

I want to sue my employer. Are there any considerations I need to keep in mind?

Yes, several. For example, depending on the kind of case, you may be required to first try to resolve the problem with your employer before resorting to a legal remedy. Second, many lawsuits have a **statute of limitations** (a time limit to file your case). If you wait too long, you may lose the right to bring your case.

I think that I was fired unfairly. Can I sue my employer for wrongful termination?

In order to sue your employer for **wrongful termination**, you'll need to prove either that you were fired illegally (e.g., out of retaliation for reporting an OSHA violation) or that your firing violated the terms of an employment agreement or other promises made to you by your employer. Your best bet would be to consult a lawyer to see if your situation would be grounds for a lawsuit in your state.

I think my supervisor is doing something illegal. I want to raise the issue with his boss, but I'm afraid I'll get fired. What should I do?

While there are ways to "blow the whistle" about your concerns without endangering your job, caution is the watchword. One good place to start is the Government Accountability Project, a nonprofit organization that advises employees who blow the whistle on wrongdoing within their organizations. Call them at 202-408-0034 or go to their Web site at **www.whistle blower.org**.

now where do I go?!

CONTACTS

U.S. Department of Labor
200 Constitution Avenue, NW
Washington, DC 20210
866-487-2365
www.dol.gov

The Occupational Safety
and Health Administration
200 Constitution Avenue, NW
Washington, DC 20210
800-321-OSHA (6742)
www.osha.gov

American Association of Retired Persons
601 E Street, NW
Washington, DC 20049
800-424-3410
www.aarp.org
—good resource for information about
age-based discrimination.

U.S. Department of Justice
950 Pennsylvania Avenue, NW
Civil Rights Division
Disability Rights Section—NYAVE
Washington, DC 20530
800-514-0301, 800-514-0383 [TDD]
www.usdoj.gov/crt/ada/adahom1.htm
—to learn more about the ADA.

Equal Employment Opportunity Commission
1801 L Street, NW
Washington, DC 20507
800-669-4000
www.eeoc.gov
—for information about antidiscrimination laws
and to file a formal complaint.

Listing of State Fair-Employment Agencies
**www.humanrights.state.mn.us/accsite/docs1
/resguide/fair_cmp.htm**

WEB SITES

www.nolo.com
—comprehensive information and answers to
commonly asked questions are provided in the
Employment Law section.

www.law.cornell.edu/topics
—an extensive online law library, maintained by
Cornell University Law School, containing summaries of each legal subject as well as links to federal and state law and other online resources.

www.freeadvice.com
—offers an extensive question and answer section
under the Employer Labor Law heading.

BOOKS

**The American Bar Association Guide to
Workplace Law**
by Barbara J. Fick

Every Employee's Guide to the Law
by Joel G. Lewin

Getting Fired
by Steven Mitchell Sack

Home

what is real estate law?

When do you need a lawyer?

Great! You're ready to purchase a home. Or maybe you've lived in your house for years and are ready to sell and trade up to a bigger place. Perhaps you've gotten an opportunity overseas and you want to rent your home out while you live abroad. In all these instances you'll run into real estate law. These laws cover everything from contracts involved in purchasing or selling a home to zoning regulations and landlord-tenant laws.

Real estate law varies greatly from state to state, and so do the situations that might require a lawyer. But the most common scenario for using a real estate lawyer is when you are buying or selling a home.

In some parts of the country, real estate lawyers are not necessary when buying or selling a home; in others, their participation is customary. To find out whether real estate lawyers are needed in the community where you are buying or selling, talk to real estate brokers, your accountant, and people you know in the area who have recently been involved in a house sale or purchase.

Hiring a real estate lawyer

To find a lawyer to help with the purchase or sale of a home, ask friends and family who have recently had a good experience with a lawyer in the community where the transaction will be taking place. Also, get referrals from your real estate broker. Accountants and other financial professionals are also good people to ask for referrals since they often deal with real estate lawyers.

How much do real estate lawyers charge?

Lawyers will charge either by the hour at a set rate or by a flat fee. Whether you pay a flat fee or by the hour, the price of the house you are purchasing or selling may affect how much you spend. The greater the value of the property, the higher the legal fees. The range should fall somewhere between $500 and $2,500, possibly higher if the transaction is complex.

Questions to ask when choosing a real estate lawyer

How many years of experience do you have?

How many real estate transactions have you handled in the area?

What are your fees? Do you charge a flat fee or by the hour? Are expenses billed separately?
Once you agree on a fee or rate, you'll want to get it in writing, something that is required by law in some states.

What is your availability during the next few months? Do you take calls after working hours?

Will you be doing the work personally, or do paralegals and legal assistants do much of the work?
If it's the latter, then the hourly fee for those paraprofessionals should be lower than the lawyer's fee.

before you sell

A little legal know-how before you leap

So you've decided to put your home on the market. The easiest way to do this is to hire a licensed real estate agent or broker. What does the agent do? First, she will help you determine the right selling price based on recent sales of local **comparable homes** (homes of similar size and construction in your neighborhood).

Once your house has been priced, the agent will write up a sales report on the house that is then available to other agents. Most agents also will host an **open house**, where other agents can come and see the house first before it officially goes on the market. After the open house, the agency will likely place ads in newspapers (at its expense) about your house. The agent will be responsible for showing your house to prospective customers.

How do you find a realtor? Nearly all real estate agents work for a real estate agency. If you don't know an agent, simply walk into a local real estate agency and ask to talk with one. While you are there, take a look at their **listings** (a list of homes for sale, noting prices, special features, and addresses). You can either choose an agent yourself or the agency will assign one to work with you. This person will be called the **listing agent**.

Selling your home yourself

You don't have to list your home with an agent in order to sell it. You can sell it yourself, which is often referred to as **for sale by owner**. If you do it yourself, you'll save on the commission charged by an agency, but you'll also be doing a lot more work—and forgoing some of the professional services a broker offers, such as placing advertisements, showing your home to prospective buyers, and handling paperwork.

Organizing Your Legal Documents

Before you put your house on the market, it's a good idea to get certain documents from your files. Some documents will be needed before your agent will officially take on selling your house, others will be needed at the closing (see page 44).

■ The deed to the house. This document proves that you were legally granted ownership of the house.

■ The title report from your closing or, if you don't have that, the title insurance policy. This document shows that you're the legal owner of the house.

■ A survey of the property—a map that shows your house and property.

■ A certificate of occupancy and any other certificates documenting work you have had done on the house. If you did extensive renovation work, you need to show that the house has been inspected and is safe for occupancy.

■ Real estate tax bills from the past two years.

■ The most recent mortgage statement.

the listing agreement

How real estate agents operate

Once you choose a real estate agent, he will ask you to sign a **listing agreement**. This is a contract between you and the real estate agency. It states how long the agent will work for you (typically 3 to 6 months) and, more important, the commission the agent will receive after selling your house. That commission is usually expressed as a percentage of the sales price and will likely be in the 3% to 6% range.

Real estate brokers generally want an **exclusive listing**, meaning they are entitled to a commission regardless of who ends up finding a buyer for the house. The other type of agreement is a **multiple listing** agreement, meaning that your house is listed on all the databases available to any real estate agent to sell. In a multiple listing situation, if an agent from an unaffiliated real estate office finds a buyer for your home, then that agent is due a portion of your agent's commission. It's a good idea to limit the contract to the shortest duration so you are not committed to staying with one broker for an unreasonable length of time. A short-term contract can also motivate a broker to sell your house faster. Another good idea is to get your broker to commit to a marketing plan in writing. That way, if he fails to properly advertise your house, you have a leg to stand on if you want to get out of the contract before the expiration date.

Make sure the listing agreement says that the broker's commission is due and payable at the **closing**—when the final paperwork is signed and payment is made.

Preferred Buyer Agreement

We will provide you with the following services:

1. We will arrange a no obligation prequalification meeting for you with a foremost home lender to find out exactly how much you qualify to borrow, and help you find the best home loan possible.

2. We will search the Multiple Listing Service for <u>all homes</u> listed by <u>all real estate companies</u> to make sure you know about every home or building site for sale in your price range, and immediately update you of new listings.

3. We will arrange private showings for any and all homes you wish to see, or arrange meetings for you with the best builders in the area.

4. We will help you with the negotiation and purchase of any "for sale by owner."

5. When you find the right home, we will assist you with preparing an offer that is in your best interests.

6. We will discuss strategy about the offer price, home loan terms, interest rates, possession date, etc.

7. We will recommend the best services: structural inspections, termite inspections, survey, appraisal, home warranty, title insurance.

8. We will obtain answers to any and all questions you may have.

9. We will present the offer on your behalf to the seller, the builder, the for sale by owner or the seller's agent. We will negotiate in your best interest at all times to get you the best deal possible.

10. We will do our best to ensure you receive exceptional service from everyone involved in the home buying process.

iDeal Location Signature:_____ Date:_____

Buyer's Signature:_____Date:_____

Buyer's Signature:_____Date:_____

ASK THE EXPERTS

My broker isn't doing a good job selling my home. Can I switch to a different agency or agent?

Once you list your property with a broker, you have to abide by your contract for its full term. For example, if you have a three-month listing agreement, you can't decide after a month to give the listing to another real estate agency—you have to wait until the listing expires. If your contract is with the agency and not a particular broker, you can ask the manager of the real estate office to assign a new agent to your home.

I've changed my mind and want to take my house off the market before the listing agreement expires. Can I do that?

Yes, but your real estate agency may expect reimbursement for advertising and other out-of-pocket costs. Also, if your broker has found a willing buyer at your price and you decide not to sell, you can be sued by the agent for damages such as lost commission or expenses incurred. You may be able to protect yourself if you insert a clause in the listing agreement that allows you to end the agreement if you change your mind about selling, or a clause that allows you to say no to any deal the broker presents to you for any reason. (However, many brokers won't agree to such conditions.)

I found a buyer myself while my house was on the market. Do I have to pay my broker anything?

You may still have to pay the broker a commission unless you and your broker agree in the listing agreement that the broker will accept a reduced commission if you find a buyer on your own.

before you buy

Know what to expect

If you want to buy a house, the first thing you have to figure out is how much you can afford to spend. Don't just consider the price of the house, but also keep in mind the monthly costs that can creep up on you (e.g., real estate taxes, utilities, repairs, and maintenance).

Once you've figured out your budget, you can start looking for houses either on your own or with the assistance of a real estate agent, also called a broker. An agent can help you find out which properties in the area are for sale and arrange for you to see them.

Keep in mind that most agents represent the seller, not the buyer, and since the agent gets paid when the house is sold, you should take the "advice" of any agent employed by the seller with a grain of salt.

In some states, however, it's common to use **buyer's brokers**, or agents who represent buyers. If you work with a buyer's broker, you will have someone looking out more for your interests. For this exclusive help, you will have to pay a commission, usually 1% to 3% of the price of the house. Depending on local norms, you may be asked to sign an exclusive agreement with a buyer's broker.

If I'm looking to buy a house, can I work with more than one real estate agency at a time?

As a buyer, you could, but there may not be any benefit to your doing so as long as you choose an agency that subscribes to the Multiple Listing Service (MLS). Because most houses are made available to all brokers on the MLS system, you should be able to see all the houses on the market that meet your criteria.

I need to buy a house quickly. How can I speed the buying process along?

Getting approved for a **mortgage** (a loan to buy a house) can take several weeks. To save time, many buyers choose to prequalify for a mortgage. This involves submitting an application to a bank and going through a credit check to get preapproved for a loan of a certain amount.

FIRST PERSON   DISASTER STORY

Inspecting the inspector

I had bought and sold a number of houses, so when I wanted to buy a new house, I figured that there was no real urgency in finding a real estate lawyer. I had a great agent, and she found the perfect house—an old Victorian. My agent recommended this inspector "who was really good with old houses." Turns out it was her brother-in-law. He rubber-stamped the inspection, never mentioning the fact that the heating system was not up to code. When I finally got around to hiring a real estate lawyer, she had heard of this inspector's sloppy record and alerted me to get another inspection. I did and was so alarmed by the problems, I retracted my offer. I realized my agent really was only interested in the sale, while my lawyer was interested in protecting me. Best to get that protection early on in the home-buying game. —Joe C.

making an offer

**On the road
to a contract**

You've found a house you like. Great. Now What?! Well, before you go out and hire a decorator, there's one minor hurdle you have to overcome—you have to make an offer (also called a **bid**) on the house, and the offer must be accepted by the seller. If you're working with a broker, your broker will help you with the bidding process.

For starters, you can either offer to pay the **listing price** (also known as the **asking price**—this is the price the house is listed at) or make an offer that is lower, depending on how competitive the market is. When you bid, you should be guided by what the house is worth to you and not be pressured by the broker to increase the price. (Remember, the more you pay for a house, the more money the broker will get in commission.)

If your price is accepted, the next step is to get something on paper reflecting the terms of your deal. In some locations, you may be asked to sign a precontract of sale, also called a **binding agreement** or **binder**. A binder is typically a form agreement prepared by the seller's broker, stating the number of days within which a contract of sale will be drafted, as well as giving an anticipated closing date. Though practice varies by locality, sometimes money is put down with a binding agreement.

While brokers often rush to get their clients to sign a binding agreement, the truth is that a binder may not be binding for either party. In fact, multiple offers are often entertained after a binder is signed. The point of a binder is to show the seller and agent that you are a serious buyer.

Is there ever a time I would want to bid more than the asking price?

There are many different philosophies on bidding, but one school of thought is that since you can always increase your bid, you may as well start out low in the hope you won't have to go higher. In a **seller's market**, when multiple buyers are interested in the same house, the seller (or his broker) may call for **sealed bids** from each prospective buyer. This is basically an auction for a house. In a sealed-bid situation, each buyer submits a bid without knowing what the other bidders are offering. The one with the highest sealed bid wins. In such cases, it may well be necessary to bid more than the listing price if you are intent on getting the house.

What is a buyer's market?

This is a term real estate agents use to describe a depressed housing market. While it's bad for the sellers, it's great for buyers because it means lower housing prices. There can many reasons for a down market; the most obvious ones are too many houses on the market at the same time, or too few buyers are interested in the houses that are for sale.

purchase agreements

Phew! You've settled on a price. Now What?! More paperwork, of course! If you are the buyer, get ready to sign a **purchase agreement** and put down more money, usually about 5% to 10% of the purchase price. This money should be held in **escrow**. That means the seller's attorney holds your money in an account that he is required to keep separate from his other funds. If all goes according to plan and you buy the house, the money in escrow will go toward the purchase price. If there's a problem and you back out of the deal, the seller can keep the money, unless there are contingencies in the agreement that weren't met (see below).

The purchase agreement has to be in writing, as verbal contracts for house sales are not enforceable. It will typically include at least the following information: the names of the buyer and seller, the purchase price, the address and tax map identification of the house (the description used for many local records), and the date of the **closing**—when you will pay the remaining portion you owe and take title to the house.

The contract will also list all items included in the sale, such as appliances, lighting fixtures, or window treatments. It will also state any **contingencies** (factors that must be fulfilled in order for the contract to go forward). Contingencies are safeguards a good lawyer will draft to ensure that the buyer can get his deposit back if there are problems. For instance, if there's a mortgage contingency, that means that if the buyer can't get a mortgage, the buyer gets his deposit money back. Or if there is an **inspection** contingency, this means that if the house doesn't pass inspection by a licensed inspector, the buyer gets her deposit back. The buyer, however, will not be refunded the cost of applying for a mortgage or for an inspection. Before you sign a purchase contract, look it over carefully and have your lawyer explain all your obligations and those of the seller.

What if the inspector finds a problem?

If you'd rather not go ahead because of any condition discovered in the inspection, you can usually back out of the deal and get your deposit back—as long as your contract includes an inspection contingency clause. You can also negotiate to lower the sale price to compensate for any repairs needed. For example, if a structural problem is found that needs to be repaired but you still want to buy the home, you may be able to convince the seller to reduce the sale price to cover the cost of repairs.

What if I change my mind and don't want the house after I've signed the contract?

You may lose all or part of your deposit if you back out at the last minute. That deposit compensates the seller for keeping the house off the market while the deal is pending and for ongoing costs.

What happens if I'm denied a mortgage?

As long as your contract has a mortgage contingency clause and you have met the terms of that clause (e.g., you have applied for a mortgage in good faith), you should be able to cancel the contract.

the deed, the title

When you buy a home, what you're really getting is **title**, or legal ownership, to the property in the form of a piece of paper called a **deed**. Before the closing, the buyer's attorney or a title company hired by the buyer will search the land records maintained by the local municipality to make sure the seller has undisputed title to the property. They do this by looking for any **liens** (claims against the property by creditors or prior owners) or mortgages on the property that will have to be satisfied in order to give the buyer clear title.

Sometimes even a competent search of the land records will not disclose a claim of ownership to the property. For this reason, it is wise (and sometimes required) for buyers to have **title insurance**, an insurance policy that protects them in the event some problem with the title to the house arises down the road (e.g., an earlier deed turns up and that owner claims title). If you're getting a mortgage, the lending bank may require that you have title insurance.

ASK THE EXPERTS

What if a title problem is discovered before the closing?

Experienced real estate lawyers are used to certain types of title problems cropping up and know how to handle them. Typical situations are old mortgages that were never paid off and prior owners dying without having their estates properly settled. In these cases, one of the attorneys (or even the title company) may hold some of the purchase money in escrow until the seller's attorney clears up the problem. The buyer's attorney will work closely with the title company to determine if the problem can be fixed. The contract should allow the buyer to back out of the deal if it can't be.

Where do I get title insurance?

Real estate attorneys and brokers generally work with one or more title insurance companies and will arrange for an insurance policy. Title insurance generally requires a one-time payment, not yearly premiums as with fire and casualty insurance.

What if I'm buying the property with someone else?

If you're buying the property with someone else, you need to decide how you want to hold title to the property—in other words, whose name will be on the deed. There are two legal concepts to consider: tenancy (the right to possess a property) and survivorship (the right to bequeath property to heirs). Typically, married couples hold as "tenants in the entirety," which means upon the death of one, the survivor becomes the outright owner. Two friends buying property usually want to take title as "tenants in common" so that each can decide who will inherit his one-half share in the property. Ask your lawyer which way is best for your needs.

What if I bought property with someone, and we can't agree about selling?

If you can't agree, and if one owner's buying out the other is not an option, then you'll have to file what is called a partition action in court against the other owner. This means that the court will supervise the sale of the property, usually at auction to the highest bidder.

the closing

Bring a new pen and lots of blank checks

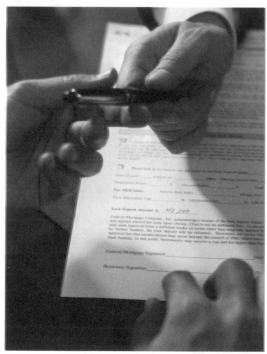

The closing is the time when the property changes hands from the seller to the buyer. It usually occurs one to two months after the purchase agreement is signed. In addition to the buyer, seller, their brokers, and maybe their attorneys, a representative from the buyer's bank and someone from the title company may attend.

Before the closing both parties should look at a **settlement statement** (a little like reviewing your hotel bill the night before checkout). This statement details what money is owed to whom and explains how various items will be handled. Also, the day before the closing the buyer should have the opportunity to do a final inspection of the house, called a **walk-through**, to see that everything is in order.

Once everyone arrives, the paperwork begins. There are numerous documents both buyer and seller need to sign. Both parties will also have to sign a few checks, some of which may need to be obtained in advance as certified checks. Among these payments are checks from the seller to the real estate agent and from the buyer to the seller; others go to the title company and to the lender for any fees associated with the loan.

The buyer gets a credit for any deposit already made on the house. There may also be adjustments for any items the seller may have prepaid such as real estate taxes or utilities covering any period after the buyer takes possession.

At the end of what will feel like a marathon session of name-signing and check-writing, the seller will give the buyer the deed and the keys to the house (plus other items mentioned in the contract, like garage door openers and alarm codes). Usually, the buyer can take possession immediately after the closing, which generally takes anywhere from one to four hours.

What kinds of things can go wrong between the signing of the contract and the closing?

Unfortunately, many things can happen. The walk-through can often turn up unexpected problems. For example, if the buyer finds something that will require significant costs to repair, both parties will be faced with the decision as to whether they should cancel the deal (assuming the condition would create proper grounds for the buyer to get out of the contract) or renegotiate the terms of the deal in light of the new discovery. Problems with financing are also common. If the buyer's financing didn't come through or didn't come through in time, the parties will have to decide whether to cancel the purchase agreement or delay the closing.

What if the seller isn't ready or able to give up the house at the time of the closing?

If the seller is in violation of a promise to deliver occupancy, then the buyer may be able to void the deal and recover his deposit and perhaps some other costs. If possession is delayed only a few days, often the parties will make cost adjustments based on the number of days involved. If the delay continues past a few days, the contract often provides for an additional penalty that the seller is charged for every day past the closing date that she fails to give possession of the property. Finally, as a last resort, the buyer can sue for what is called **specific performance**. This means the buyer can attempt to force the seller to go through with the sale and hand over the property.

building from scratch or renovating

Real estate law still applies

So you've bought a piece of property and now you want to build your dream house. Or, you've been living in your house for years and finally saved enough to put on an addition. Either way, you'll need to find a builder (also called a **contractor**) and/or an architect to do the work. There are important things to consider when drawing up contracts with these professionals.

If the work you're doing is aesthetic rather than structural (e.g., resurfacing the kitchen cabinets as opposed to building a new bathroom), you will probably just hire a contractor. If you're making structural changes, you may also need an architect. Before hiring anyone, ask to see examples of work they have

done and get references. And when you interview former clients, don't be shy about asking whether the architect and builder adhered to the budget and schedule, and whether their crews left a mess at the end of each working day.

You can also check up on construction professionals through the local Better Business Bureau or Department of Consumer Affairs. Construction work often requires dealing with municipal boards and other local governing bodies, and you want to be confident that your team will be able to get the necessary permits and zoning approvals to do your project.

When you have an entire house built for you, you must enter into a construction agreement with the builder. Contracts for a home that is being built to your specifications are very precise as to materials to be used and other details.

Tips for Dealing with Contractors and Architects

Once you've found the contractor and/or architect, here are some issues to consider.

■ **Construction contracts**—Your contractor will want you to sign a contract that stipulates, among other things, the work to be done and the payment for it. If it's a big job, it's smart to have a real estate lawyer review it for you. A lawyer can make sure the contract protects you in case of default or poor performance by the contractor.

■ **Developing a payment schedule**—Your contractor will want as much payment in advance as possible, but you'll want to delay payments to ensure that the contractor will do the work on schedule and finish the job. It's best to provide enough money up front to cover the contractor's building and material expenses, but hold out a major payment until the project is completed.

■ **Inspecting the work**—Your architect can act as an inspector for what the contractor is doing (e.g., using the right materials, following the architectural plans). Some states require on-site inspections by your town's building inspector.

■ **Obtaining permits**—Certain certificates of completion are issued by the local municipality after work is completed, and as the homeowner, you will need to show all such certificates when you go to sell your house. It's a good idea to tie the final payments to the receipt of all necessary certificates of approval.

■ **Hiring subcontractors**—Make sure your contract states how subcontractors are to be paid. You'll also want to get releases (sometimes called **lien waivers**) from any subcontractors after they complete their work and have been paid. This will protect you from a subcontractor's putting a **lien** on your house (a claim on a piece of property to secure payment for a debt) in the event that the contractor hasn't properly paid his subcontractors.

renters and landlords

If you want to rent out your apartment or house, or if you want to rent an apartment from a landlord, there are some basic things you should know about the landlord-tenant relationship. This is another area of the law that varies by state, so if you get into a thorny situation, you will likely need to consult a lawyer who specializes in landlord-tenant matters in your locality.

Whether you're a renter or landlord, it's wise to have the legal protection and clarity afforded by a **lease**, a written contract that addresses the duties and obligations of each party. Simple leases are sold in stationery stores. Many people use these leases as a starting point that can be modified by adding **riders** (addenda to cover unique arrangements between the parties).

Duties of a Landlord

As a landlord, once you rent a space to a tenant, you'll need to turn over the keys and understand that you can no longer enter the dwelling without the tenant's permission, unless there is an emergency. You're expected to maintain the dwelling in a safe and habitable condition (e.g., keeping the roof in good repair and the heating system in working condition).

Duties of a Tenant

Your primary obligation as a tenant is to pay the rent in a timely fashion, but you will also generally agree not to damage the property or conduct illegal activities on the premises. If you fail to meet obligations stipulated in the lease, the landlord may evict you from the premises. Eviction is a complicated legal process that varies by state—but in all instances, the landlord must follow certain procedures and can't just lock you out without notice.

What are the rules governing security deposits?

When signing a lease, a tenant is required to pay a security deposit (usually one or two months' rent), which provides the landlord with money to cover any costs if the tenant defaults on the rent or causes damage. Landlords are generally required to keep security deposits in a special account and turn over the yearly interest to the tenant. When the tenant leaves, the landlord is obligated to refund the security deposit, less any portion needed for repair of damages caused by the tenant. If the landlord fails to return the security deposit or can't account for repairs made with it, the tenant can sue in housing or small claims court.

What if my tenant's damages exceed the security deposit?

It's a good idea to have some proof of the condition of the premises before the tenant moves in (either by taking photos or by having the tenant acknowledge the condition of the premises in the lease). To cover the damages, you'll have to sue the tenant. You'll need to provide proof, so you should take photos of the wreckage before repairs are made, and you should keep all receipts.

What if I have tenants in my apartment, but I want to sell it or use it for myself?

When a tenant signs a lease, she's usually fully protected for the term of the lease. So unless the tenant has violated the lease (in which case the tenant can be evicted), you're stuck until the end date of the lease. If you're selling your property, you're going to have to deal with the tenants before you sign a purchase and sale agreement. Don't set a closing date based on an optimistic assessment of how quickly you can evict the tenants. If they're still in the dwelling on the closing day, you may be in breach of your contract to the buyer. One option is to see if the tenants would be interested in a buyout, a deal in which you would pay them a certain amount to be released from the lease.

homeowner's insurance and liability

Make sure you're covered

Homeowner's insurance covers the cost of any repairs or replacements needed in your home due to fire or theft (and in some cases, natural disasters like earthquakes or floods). For this coverage, you pay the insurance company a fee or **premium**. Homeowner's insurance is generally required by banks or lenders as part of the condition of getting a mortgage to buy a house.

Homeowner's insurance also covers you if someone is injured on your property, including friends and family, tradespeople, delivery people, and solicitors. Depending on the facts of the situation, your homeowner's insurance company may defend you and pay monetary damages if any of these people make a claim against you for injuries. But note, insurance coverage is no guarantee that you'll be completely absolved of financial responsibility.

As with all insurance, your premium will increase with the number of claims made against you. It's a good idea to review your insurance coverage every year or so, particularly if you've made a major purchase or improvements to your home. You may need to increase the amount of coverage, which will increase your monthly premium as well.

ASK THE EXPERTS

I told my neighbor not to pet my dog, but she did and he bit her. Am I liable for her medical bills?

It all depends on the facts and circumstances surrounding the incident. There are many factors that would determine liability in the event your neighbor sued, such as if you knew your dog was vicious (e.g., he had attacked before) and you let the dog run loose. A court may also look at whether your neighbor provoked or taunted the dog in some way.

The postal carrier slipped on my walkway delivering the mail. Will I be held responsible for her injuries?

As a homeowner, you have a responsibility to use reasonable care in maintaining your property and to warn those who come onto the property of known hazards. Whether you would be held responsible for her injuries would depend on whether you contributed to the accident (e.g., by failing to clear an icy walkway), whether the postal carrier was careless, or whether it was just an accident that was no one's fault. Regardless of who is considered to be at fault, your homeowner's policy may cover this type of accident—if so, your insurance company may provide you with a lawyer to defend you in the event you are sued. Call your insurance broker to find out.

What if I don't own my own home? Would it be a good idea to get rental insurance?

Yes, renter's insurance will cover the loss of your valuables should they be stolen or damaged from a natural disaster.

now what do I do?
Answers to common questions

There are certain covenants in the neighborhood association. Are they legally binding?

Covenants are rules put into place by communities to ensure that certain standards are met in a neighborhood (mostly having to do with matters of aesthetics). For example, a covenant may restrict the homeowner's ability to erect a satellite dish if that is felt to be unsightly by the association's governing body. While covenants aren't laws, they're enforceable by the association. If you violate them, your homeowners' association may be able to sue you—so if you are buying a home in a community with by-laws or other restrictions, make sure you're familiar with the rules before you buy.

I'm buying a house directly from the owner. What do I need to do to protect myself?

If there's no broker involved, the seller may just supply you with a standard contract of sale, which you should take to your lawyer to review. If the seller isn't represented by a lawyer, be careful about how your deposit is handled. See if you can have the deposit held in escrow by your lawyer.

I'm a landlord, and I think my tenant is running an illegal business out of the apartment she rents from me. What can I do about it?

Call the police and let them handle it—and do that as soon as possible. If your tenant is running a criminal enterprise, that will likely be grounds for eviction. Either way, you must report it first to find out.

I have a roommate who is subletting from me, and she has been late on her rent for 3 months. Is there anything I can do to force her to pay?

Many subletting arrangements involve leases, and if so, the lease should outline the same responsibilities as those between you and your landlord (with you now playing the landlord role and your subletter as the tenant). If there is no written agreement or lease, it will be harder to collect, but you can always go into court—possibly even on your own without the assistance of a lawyer—even if all you have is an oral agreement. Be prepared for an argument that will likely come down to your word against hers.

now where do I go?!

CONTACTS

www.findlaw.com—legal portal with content customized to legal professionals, students, the public, and businesses. In the "Public" section, look under "Housing" for real estate resources.

www.homepath.com—information about buying a home and obtaining a mortgage, including rate calculators that help you figure out how much you can afford to borrow.

Housing Resources—**www.gsa.gov**—a collection of booklets from the Federal Consumer Information Center related to buying, financing, and maintaining a house.

www.realtor.com—a comprehensive database of homes available for sale, sponsored by the National Association of Realtors.

National Association of Realtors
www.realtor.com, 800-874-6500—trade association of the real estate industry.

BOOKS

100 Questions Every First-Time Home Buyer Should Ask
by Ilyce R. Glink

The 90-Second Lawyer Guide to Buying Real Estate
by Robert Irwin and David L. Ganz

Your New House: The Alert Consumer's Guide to Buying and Building a Quality Home
by Alan Fields and Denise Fields

Every Tenant's Legal Guide
by Janet Portman
(Editors Mary Randolph
and Ralph E. Warner)

Landlording: A Handy Manual for Scrupulous Landlords and Landladies Who Do It Themselves
by Leigh Robinson

Family Law

Mr. and Mrs. Andrew Colgate
of Dartmouth, Massachusetts,
announce the engagement
of their daughter,

Kimberly Ann,
to
Kevin Henry Taylor,

son of

s. Adam T

pton Cr

Hamp

lding

what is family law?

Hiring a lawyer

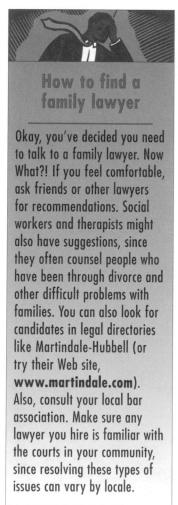

How to find a family lawyer

Okay, you've decided you need to talk to a family lawyer. Now What?! If you feel comfortable, ask friends or other lawyers for recommendations. Social workers and therapists might also have suggestions, since they often counsel people who have been through divorce and other difficult problems with families. You can also look for candidates in legal directories like Martindale-Hubbell (or try their Web site, **www.martindale.com**). Also, consult your local bar association. Make sure any lawyer you hire is familiar with the courts in your community, since resolving these types of issues can vary by locale.

It's not that love is blind, but that formalizing a love affair into a legal relationship can be a real eye-opener. Getting married and having children can be fraught with difficulties, and along the way you may find you need legal advice. If so, find a lawyer who specializes in **family law**, also known as **matrimonial law**.

The first thing that comes to mind when you think about family law is probably divorce, but family lawyers are on the scene for more than just breakups. If you want to talk about the financial implications of getting married or moving in with someone, you would consult one. Or if you were involved in a same-sex relationship and wanted to explore the legality of getting married or entering into a cohabitation agreement, a family lawyer would be able to help. Adoption is another scenario that involves family lawyers. Other possible needs: paternity, child support, custody and visitation, prenuptial agreements, and restraining orders.

So once you know you need to see one, where do you find a family lawyer? The best way is to get a referral from a friend or family member. Note: Family law also touches on issues of estate planning, and often these two areas overlap (e.g., appointing a guardian for children, distribution of assets during a divorce), so as you're thinking about these issues, also take a look at the chapter on wills and trusts (see page 152).

Questions to Ask in an Interview with a Family Lawyer

When you meet with a family lawyer, you will likely be talking about some of the most personal issues in your life. For that reason, it's very important that you feel comfortable with the person you hire. Be wary of a lawyer who gives you the hard sell and/or promises a certain result. And before you hire anyone, it's a good idea to interview a few lawyers first.

What percentage of your practice is devoted to matrimonial law, and how long have you been doing it?
Also ask if they have expertise in any unusual aspects of your case.

What is your policy on returning phone calls (e.g,. will you return calls within 24 hours)?
Sometimes you will be upset, and even if your lawyer is unavailable, you will want a callback whether it's from an assistant or a paralegal.

Do you provide a written retainer agreement, and what is the standard fee structure?
Family law is generally an area with hourly billing. Make sure to ask whether bills will be itemized and what happens if you settle your case before the retainer is used up.

What if you and your spouse own a business together?
If you're going through a divorce and a business or other complex financial tax aspects are involved, ask if the lawyer has experience valuing business interests and is familiar with the tax implications of divorce.

How do you feel about mediation?
Mediation (where the parties meet with a third party, who helps them come to an agreement or recommends a settlement in the case) is often a less adversarial setting than court, and depending on your case, you may want a lawyer who encourages mediation rather than battling everything out in court (which gets very costly, both emotionally and financially).

marriage

Happily ever after—hopefully . . .

You meet. You fall in love. And before long, you're registering for china and toaster ovens. Surprisingly, embarking on the life event that will most dramatically change your legal status doesn't require the services of a lawyer at all. Depending on where you live, you'll likely need to obtain a marriage license, take a blood test, and of course go through any specific procedures required by your religion. However, while it's very easy to enter into a marriage, it's very difficult to get out of one, especially if there are children and/or significant financial assets.

One way to make a possible divorce easier is to enter into a **prenuptial agreement**, a legally binding agreement signed before marriage that dictates how assets are to be distributed in the event of divorce. Often people enter prenuptial agreements when there's a great disparity of income between the two parties or when one person has an ownership interest in a preexisting or family-owned business. Prenups, as they're called, are also common in second (or third or fourth!) marriages when the people getting married are older and have children or grandchildren whom they want to make sure are financially protected. For a prenup, you will need a lawyer.

His   Hers

ASK THE EXPERTS

My future wife's family says their family lawyer will take care of a prenuptial agreement for both of us. Is that okay?

No, it's not okay. In fact, the agreement will very likely not be enforceable if you both use the same lawyer.

My fiancé won't marry me if I insist on a prenup, and I don't want to lose him. What else I can do?

There are ways besides a prenup to protect premarital, gifted, and inherited assets (e.g., by keeping such assets separated and in your own name during the marriage). Make sure to discuss these issues with a lawyer.

Are there situations when a prenuptial agreement would not be considered valid in court?

There are many issues that arise in prenups and many grounds upon which these agreements can be challenged as invalid. For example, there must be full financial disclosure between the two parties, the details must be worked out far enough in advance of the wedding so that the agreement does not seem coercive, each party should have independent counsel, and the agreement can't be too one-sided. If your fiancé is the one insisting on a prenup, make sure that you fully understand exactly what you're being asked to give up (e.g., what your rights would be under the law if you didn't have a prenup). Also keep in mind that waiver of alimony clauses in prenups often don't stand up in court.

Legal implications of marriage

While the nuances of marital law vary from state to state, these are some of the ways your legal rights will be affected by getting married:

- **Inheritance rights** unless there is a prenuptial agreement or other waiver of inheritance rights, a spouse is entitled by law to a share of the deceased spouse's property.

- **Government benefits** spouses have rights to each other's pension and unemployment benefits unless they waive these rights.

- **Property** spouses are entitled to an interest in property and assets acquired during the marriage.

- **Taxes** married couples are entitled to file a joint tax return, which is generally but not always a benefit. Married couples who file a joint tax return are also held responsible for taxes incurred by their spouses.

- **Debts** married couples are liable for certain of each other's debts.

- **Support** married couples have a legal duty to support each another financially.

living together

**What rights
do you have?**

Okay, you've been living together and you don't want to get married. But you would like to make a stronger commitment to your partner and extend some of the rights and privileges of marriage to each other. What do you do?

For these reasons and others, some unmarried couples decide to formalize their relationship with a written contract, sometimes called a **cohabitation agreement**. Usually, these agreements specify financial issues, such as who is responsible for what shares of expenses. However, family lawyers have seen all kinds of weird things covered in these agreements (watch out for someone who wants to put your responsibility to make the bed into a contract!). These agreements also state what happens should the relationship end—for example, who has to move out, how a sale of property would work if a jointly owned home is involved, and who owns the items you each brought into the relationship and acquired while together.

In addition to a cohabitation agreement, there are other ways to indicate your wishes and extend the rights of a significant other. Some examples: You can give someone a **power of attorney** (a right to act on your behalf in situations that you specify, such as the right to sign your name on legal documents or have access to your banking or checking account); grant a **durable power of attorney for healthcare** or **healthcare proxy** (which would allow your significant other to make health decisions on your behalf if you are unable to); set up joint bank accounts; revise your will to acknowledge your partner; name your partner as a beneficiary of an insurance policy; or purchase real estate together, taking title with rights of **survivorship**. (See chapter 8 for more details.)

ASK THE EXPERTS

I've been living with a guy for 15 years, and now he's involved with someone else. Can I sue for alimony? Am I entitled to any assets he acquired during the relationship?

Depending on the circumstances, you may be entitled to something, particularly if he introduced you to friends and family as his wife or made statements saying he would always support you (preferably in writing or with other witnesses around). Such payments, called **palimony**, are not recognized by all states. If your state recognizes **common law marriage**, you'll have a better chance. In common law marriage states, people who cohabitate for a certain number of years or meet other criteria are treated as if they are legally married. If your state doesn't recognize common law marriage, you may be out of luck, unless your assets are owned in both your names.

I'm gay and I want to get married. How can I find out if it's legal in my state?

Very few states offer same-sex couples the right to get married. However, in states where they are recognized, **domestic partnership agreements**—arrangements that provide some of the benefits of marriage to unmarried couples—are an option for same-sex couples. To learn more about domestic partnerships, contact the Marriage Project of the Lambda Legal Defense and Education Fund, 212-809-8585, **www.lambdalegal.org**.

My wife has a big pension. We're fighting, and I'm nervous that she'll remove me as the beneficiary of this pension. Can she do this?

Unless you specifically waive your rights, as a spouse you are generally protected by law as the beneficiary of a pension that has death benefits.

annulment and separation

What happens when marriages are on the rocks?

Papers to bring

When you schedule your first meeting with a lawyer, he should tell you what to bring. It's a good idea to have these items handy:

- Three years of tax returns
- Personal financial statement
- Pay stubs
- Retirement statements
- Bank account statements

It's a well-known fact that one out of every two marriages ends in divorce. So before you marry, it's a good idea to know a little something about what will happen in the event your marriage winds up on the unfortunate side of that statistic. If a married couple is ready to call it quits, there are a few different things that can happen.

If the decision to dissolve the marriage happens early on in the marriage, you can try to get an **annulment**, which is basically a legal procedure that erases the marriage. Annulments are very rarely granted and then only for very specific reasons. Even if you get an annulment, there still may be property issues to address if you've jointly acquired assets.

What if you know the marriage is not working, but you're not sure about whether you want to divorce? Your first step should be to get marital counseling. If that doesn't work, a **separation** may be the way to go. However, beware—being separated has varying legal relevance depending on the state where you live. In some states, the advantage to having a period of separation before divorce is that it can constitute grounds for a **no-fault divorce**, a legal nicety that just means your ultimate divorce may happen more easily or quickly. When there are children involved, couples often enter into a written separation agreement, which outlines how they expect to share financial and custodial responsibility for the children. Since separation agreements can set a precedent for how these things will be handled in a divorce, it's wise to get lawyers involved to write one.

What are examples of grounds for a civil annulment?

A marriage might be annulled if one person was still married to someone else at the time of a second marriage; lied about something critical to the marriage, such as a willingness to have children or the ability to have children; was of limited mental capacity; or had judgment compromised by alcohol or drugs at the time of the marriage so that she didn't understand what she was doing.

FIRST PERSON   DISASTER STORY

Annulment 101

I had only been married for 3 months when my spouse announced that he had no interest in ever having children. I was crushed. I didn't know what to do. After much soul-searching I decided to get a divorce. I found a lawyer in the phone book who filed the divorce for me. What she didn't mention was that I could have gotten a civil annulment. I wish I had investigated that legal option because my religion doesn't approve of divorce. —Carol M.

divorce

A divorce is technically a lawsuit one spouse files against another. Historically, it was only possible to get a divorce if one party did something wrong, and the reasons for the divorce (called **grounds**) had to be spelled out in the legal complaint (e.g., adultery or desertion). Today, in most states it's possible to get a **no-fault divorce**, which allows a couple to end a marriage much more simply and without assigning fault to either one. In a no-fault divorce, the person seeking the divorce (or both of them if the decision is mutual) would cite something like **irreconcilable differences** or **a year or more of separation** as the grounds for divorce, depending on what the state law allows.

Regardless of the grounds, a divorce can only become final when a court renders a decision or the two people come to an agreement on how they're going to address issues of property distribution, **alimony** (support payments to a spouse after marriage), and **child custody** and support. The least painful route to a divorce (from both a financial and an emotional perspective) is to work out the details of a divorce agreement and then file a no-fault complaint. If that isn't possible, and grounds are alleged in a divorce complaint, the process can become messy. If your lawyer recommends that you begin your divorce with a hostile complaint, make sure to ask why, especially if you think that you and your spouse will be able to work things out in a more amicable fashion, as through negotiations or mediation.

If the people involved can't come to an agreement or one side needs immediate court relief (e.g., one person moved out and took all the couple's money), then there will be no option but to have a lawyer file a complaint, citing grounds, in order to get the court involved immediately. The grounds cited in a divorce complaint are often a legal formality and will not have any bearing on the ultimate resolution of the case, except in extreme circumstances.

My lawyer seems extremely chummy with my wife's lawyer. Should I be concerned?

Lawyers are completely capable of having a social relationship with adversaries and it should not affect how they represent their clients. In fact, a friendly relationship between opposing lawyers sometimes helps speed negotiations. But if this is bothering you, talk to your lawyer about it.

How long will it take to get a divorce?

If you work out an agreement, a divorce can often be processed in one to two months (though some states require that you and your spouse live apart for a certain length of time as well). With no agreement, it can take much longer, even years, as you await a trial date.

We're getting divorced, but we're broke and trying to save what little money there is. Should we both use the same lawyer?

Absolutely not! Divorce, even an amicable one, has adversarial aspects to it, and you must each have your own attorney to advise you. Hire two lawyers, but have one of them do most of the work (e.g., drafting of documents), and then split the cost of both lawyers. This should save time and money because the one who did less work will charge less.

Can I avoid a lawyer and a divorce agreement?

If you and your spouse earn similar amounts of money, have no issues of property distribution or alimony (meaning neither will be providing continued support to the other), and no children, some states offer simplified uncontested divorce packets. Consult your local bar association or local court clerk. But a divorce with no complications is very rare—and you would be wise to have at least one consultation with a lawyer.

What about mediation?

There is a growing movement toward using alternatives to legal action in divorce cases. One of the most popular options is mediation, which involves both spouses meeting with a neutral person trained to help them come to an agreement that is mutually acceptable.

Though a lawyer is typically not present at a mediation, your lawyer can prepare you beforehand, and you can review any proposed agreement with your lawyer before you sign it.

An advantage of mediation is that it lowers your legal fees. It may also save you time if the courts in your area are backed up.

Mediation is confidential and nonbinding, which means that you won't be committed to following the mediator's recommendation. However, it's not appropriate for all cases, so make sure to ask your lawyer about your situation.

property distributions

Who gets what

As you dismantle your married life, you'll need to go through the difficult process of deciding how to divide the property you've acquired during the marriage. This division process can be worked out in several different ways: amicably in negotiations with your spouse (sometimes with both your lawyers present); through mediation; or in the courts, where a judge will apply laws that govern how marital property gets distributed in a divorce. Even after divorce, families continue to be families, especially when there are children involved. Because **litigation** (legal action) can be hostile, mediation may be a good chance for the couple to develop a way of interacting with each other that will be useful in handling coparenting issues and the inevitable family events that will follow down the road. If your case gets decided in court, the distribution of your property will follow the standards of the state where you live. Some states use a model called **community property**—which means that if property was acquired during the marriage, through the efforts of either person, it belongs equally to each one. In such states, each person will be entitled to exactly half of the marital property, regardless of the grounds for divorce.

The majority of states follow a different model, called **equitable distribution** (also called **separate property**), which means property distribution is determined on a case-by-case basis. The philosophy of equitable distribution is to look at what is fair in a particular marriage. Some of the factors that come into play are the length of the marriage and whether it was a first marriage, the contribution of the people involved, and the type of assets. Note that when courts look at who contributed what, raising children and supporting a spouse's career advancement are considered.

How is the marital property divided?

The property is rarely physically divided. Rather, an asset such as a home is valued by an appraiser and each party gets a portion of the value. This often involves selling the property and dividing the proceeds. Certain types of property are not part of the distribution. (For example, money one person received through a gift or inheritance that was never co-mingled into assets held in both names.)

Do I have to give back the engagement ring?

The law often draws a distinction between gifts given before the marriage and gifts given during the marriage. If it was a gift before marriage, the ring might be deemed yours rather than marital property, and therefore not one of the assets to be divided.

How do I know what assets we have? My spouse keeps track of all those, and I'm in the dark.

There's a process called **discovery** in which your lawyer can insist upon answers and documentation relating to assets. Under the rules of discovery, answers have to be given under oath and all relevant documents must be produced. Besides property you can see and touch, some examples of assets are 401(k)s, pensions, stock options, and insurance policies.

What do I need to consider if my husband and I own a business together?

If a divorce involves valuing business interests such as a medical practice or a family business, use a lawyer who is experienced in those kinds of cases. A good lawyer will also be sensitive to the tax implications of trading certain assets for others, something that arises when the assets being distributed are complex. It's often necessary to hire a business appraiser to value your spouse's business. Whenever possible, both sides should consider using the same expert, to ensure neutrality.

Tax aspects of divorce

The tax implications of divorce are very important, so you'll want to review them carefully with your lawyer as well as an accountant, particularly if you have extensive assets.

A few things to keep in mind: alimony is tax deductible to the recipient; child support and distribution of property are generally tax neutral to either party.

Be careful if you are dividing assets such as stock, because of the capital gains tax implications. Even custody issues will have tax implications—often a parent without custody of the children may want, for tax reasons, to be able to declare one of the children as a dependent under a divorce agreement.

alimony

Supporting the ex

The division of property isn't the end of the money talk during a divorce. When a marriage ends, one person often provides continued financial support to the other in the form of payments called **alimony** or **spousal support**. Traditionally, it was the husband who paid alimony to the wife, but with the rise of dual-income couples, generally support is paid by the spouse who's the bigger wage earner.

Alimony can be temporary or permanent. Temporary alimony (also called **term alimony**) ends after a certain period of time—generally long enough for the recipient to build up himself or herself financially. Permanent alimony typically ceases when the recipient remarries or either party dies, or the court ends support at some later point in time (as when the person who is paying alimony retires).

When it comes to determining alimony, a court will consider a number of factors, including the standard of living enjoyed during the marriage, the earning capabilities of the two people, the length of the marriage, and the health and age of those involved.

Even after alimony is set, it's important to realize that it's subject to review and can be modified or terminated in the event of changed circumstances for either person. For example, if the paying spouse loses her job or runs into a health problem that affects her earning ability, it's likely that she'd be able to reduce or end her support payments. Similarly, if the spouse being supported receives a large inheritance or wins the lottery, alimony payments would be adjusted. Parties can agree to make spousal support nonmodifiable if they choose.

ASK THE EXPERTS

My husband holds a Ph.D. in chemistry but has refused to work for the last 5 years. Now he wants alimony. Will I have to pay?

A court will calculate the earning potential of a person seeking alimony based on his education, work experience, ability to work, etc. Whether you have to pay alimony will depend on whether there is a great difference between what you earn and what your husband could earn. The less difference there is, the less likely it is that you will have to pay.

Do I have to pay my wife alimony if she left me for another guy?

Unfortunately, you still might. It's one factor some courts may consider—but a more significant factor is her need and your ability to pay. Other factors are whether she's living with the man, whether he is supporting her, and whether she'd be using your alimony to support him. This would typically be decided by a court hearing.

I receive alimony from my husband. What happens if he dies?

The spouse receiving support payments should make sure there's some security in place, like life insurance, to ensure that if the paying spouse dies, the surviving spouse will receive some kind of lump-sum payment. Alimony ends absolutely upon death.

Health insurance

Health insurance is often tied to one spouse's employment; in such cases, it's common for the support obligation to include payments for contributing to the cost of medical insurance.

It's also sometimes possible to extend coverage to a former spouse under COBRA (a federal law called the Consolidated Omnibus Reconciliation Act) for 3 years following a divorce, so if you're nervous about medical benefits, this is something you should look into.

custody and child support

How it works

If there are children involved in a divorce, you'll need to determine who has responsibility for them (in legal terms this is called **custody**). The law splits this responsibility into two components: **legal custody**, which means responsibility for decisions involving health, welfare, and education; and **physical custody**, which is responsibility for day-to-day care.

As with other elements of a divorce, custody will be decided through negotiation with lawyers, mediation, or in court. In all instances, the guiding principle will be what is in the **best interests** of the children. Depending on their age, children's preferences may be taken into account, but they're not the determining factor since courts realize that children are often influenced by one parent.

Each type of custody can be assumed by one of the spouses (**sole physical custody** or **sole legal custody**) or shared in some manner by both (**joint physical** or **joint legal custody**). In many cases, one spouse will have primary physical or residential custody of the children and both parents will share joint legal custody. In such cases, the noncustodial spouse will have **visitation** rights, which means that the spouse can take the children according to a well-defined schedule (e.g., alternate weekends, part of the summer vacation, and certain holidays). Joint physical custody is not as common, because it requires that the parents live near each other and can maintain a friendly relationship.

Historically, when looking at the best interests of children, the law favored mothers over fathers. There's still some belief in a doctrine called the **tender years presumption**—that in the case of an equally good mother and father, it's assumed that a child is better off with the mother, particularly if the child is under the age of 6. These days, courts recognize that gender roles are changing, but this assumption still influences many judges in their decisions.

If my ex is not current in his child support payments, can I refuse to let him see the children?

No. Deadbeat parents, as they are called in the press, don't lose their rights to see their children.

Will my husband be forced to contribute to the cost of a college education for our child?

It depends upon his income and the requirements of your state. In some states parental support obligations end after the child finishes high school. In other states, parents are expected to contribute toward a college education.

Will the fact that my spouse committed adultery have any impact on whether I get custody of the kids?

Not necessarily. The law accepts the notion that it's possible to be a good parent without being a good spouse. However, if the adultery directly affects someone's ability to be a good parent (e.g., going out on dates every night), courts will certainly take that into account.

I'm sick of paying a lawyer to take my ex to court every time he fails to pay child support. Are there any other alternatives?

One option is to require that the support be paid through your state's enforcement agency, which may be the district attorney's office or the probation department. That way you can have his wages **garnished** (part of his salary automatically directed to you to cover the support payments).

Child support

By law, both parents are obligated to contribute financially to the care and well-being of their children. This generally means the noncustodial parent must make payments, called child support, to the custodial parent. In most cases, the payments continue until the child reaches the legal age of majority, which is generally 18.

Most states have guidelines for calculating child support. Factors include the age of the children, their needs, the earnings of each parent, and the number of nights the children spend in each home.

If a man fathers a child out of wedlock, he has the same financial obligations as he would if he and the mother were married. If the man doesn't provide support, the mother can file a paternity suit against him, demanding that he meet his support obligations.

adoption

The decision to adopt a child, or to give a child up for adoption, is a personal and emotional choice, but it's also highly regulated by state law. If you're exploring adoption, it would be wise to find a lawyer who specializes in this area. Adoptions are handled in two different ways—**privately** and through **adoption agencies**—and the route you choose will affect many aspects of the process.

With an agency adoption, it is generally easier to know at the outset what the process will entail, since it is highly controlled by the agency. Private adoptions can be more expensive and complicated than agency adoptions, but for some people they are preferred or are the only option available. In a private adoption, the adoptive parents locate the child they eventually adopt. They might do this by placing ads in newspapers or by spreading the word in their community.

Since state laws vary on adoption issues (e.g., the amount of money that can be exchanged, the legality of advertising, whether a birth mother has a long period of time in which she can change her mind about the adoption, etc.), you should consult a lawyer knowledgeable about the laws in the area where you're seeking to locate a child.

In either situation, it's illegal to purchase a baby. While an adoptive parent can cover certain expenses for a birth mother (such as medical expenses or necessary travel), making additional payments can result in trouble for both the adopting parents and the birth mother—and may be considered a crime.

ASK THE EXPERTS

I'm unmarried, but I have a stable job with good benefits and will be able to afford childcare. Will the fact that I'm single work against me if I try to adopt?

It may make placement a bit more difficult, but adoptions into single-parent households are a growing trend.

What if I adopt a baby and the birth mother changes her mind? Are there any circumstances in which I'd have to give up the baby?

Yes, if the mother hasn't entirely surrendered her rights, this could happen. State law varies on this issue, but many states provide a birth mother with a time period in which she can change her mind. That period can range from 48 hours to as much as a year. For this reason and others, it's very important that your lawyer be familiar with the law of the state where the baby is being born.

If I adopt a baby, will the birth mother be able to contact her later?

This depends on the terms of the adoption and whether it was open or closed. In an **open adoption**, the adoptive parents agree that there can be communication between the birth mother and the child. In a **closed adoption**, the parties agree that there will be no communication; in fact, the birth mother may not know the identities of the adoptive parents. Both types of adoption are legal; it's up to the people involved to decide which they prefer. Keep in mind that fathers have the same rights as mothers, so if the father's identity is known, both parents will need to surrender their rights to the child.

now what do I do?
Answers to common questions

My wife has told me that if I don't agree to her financial demands in a settlement, she's going to call the police and claim that I hit her, have me removed from the house, and get sole custody of our daughter. What can I do to protect myself?

Unfortunately the domestic violence laws are occasionally misused as a tool to gain an advantage in a heavily contested divorce. Avoid confrontations with your wife and leave the residence if she starts an argument.

I'm worried my ex-husband is neglecting the kids when he has them for his weekend. Can I ask the court to only allow supervised visits?

If the custodial parent fears for the child's safety when visiting with the noncustodial parent and can prove neglect, it might be possible to arrange for supervised visitation, which means that the visits can only take place in the presence of another authorized adult, generally a family friend or a relative.

How can I find an adoption agency?

If you're interested in working with an adoption agency, there are several ways to locate one. Since state law regulates adoption agencies, your state Department of Health and Human Services will have a list of all licensed agencies in your area. The National Adoption Information Clearinghouse is a federally funded resource covering all aspects of adoption. For information, visit **www.calib.com/naic** or call 703-352-3488 or 888-251-0075. Adoption lawyers will also know the names of agencies. Religious institutions and hospitals may also be good places for referrals, since they often help a birth mother find a suitable home for an unplanned child.

My lawyer went into court opposing my wife's application for temporary support and lost; now I have to pay a high support that I can't afford. If I hire a new attorney, can that decision be reversed?

Unless your original lawyer made some egregious error (e.g., misrepresenting the figures), it's extremely unlikely that a judge will change his mind.

Will I have to pay my wife's attorney fees?

Attorney fees are like alimony. Typically the high earner makes a contribution to the lower earner's fees, unless the lower earner receives so much money through equitable distribution that this is deemed unnecessary.

now where do I go?!

CONTACTS

National Domestic Violence Hotline, 800-799-SAFE (7233) or **www.ndvh.org**—a national organization that provides 24-hour, 7-day-a-week assistance and information to victims of domestic violence.

American Academy of Adoption Attorneys, 202-832-2222 or **www.adoptionattorneys. org**—this national association of adoption attorneys provides a list of adoption attorneys by state.

www.findlaw.com—offers legal information. In the "Public" section, look under "Family."

BOOKS

A Smart Divorce: A Practical Guide to the 200 Things You Must Know
by Susan T. Goldstein
and Valerie H. Colb

Divorce Handbook
by James T. Friedman

What Everywoman should know about Divorce and Custody
by Gayle Rosenwald Smith
and Sally Abrahms

Your Car

you, your car, and the law

Getting local legal help

If you're like most people, a car is one of the most expensive purchases you'll make in your life. And with that big expenditure could come some thorny situations. Between accidents, traffic violations, and plain old car problems, it's obvious that your dealings with this giant machine can affect your pocketbook, your health, and even your liberty. In some instances, you may find yourself in search of a lawyer to help untangle you from a mess.

Often, one of the first things you need to figure out is whether you actually need a lawyer or if the problem is something you can handle on your own or with your insurance company. Depending on the issue you're facing, you'd use different types of lawyers. For example, you'd use a personal-injury lawyer (see page 94) if you were the victim in a car accident. But if you caused an accident after you'd been drinking, you may need a criminal lawyer (see pages 114–115).

However, if you are fighting a ticket for speeding, failing to stop at a stop sign, or some other minor violation, you generally don't need a lawyer to represent you in traffic court. One exception is if your driver's license is in jeopardy because you've amassed multiple moving violations; in that case, it would be wise to find a lawyer familiar with your local traffic court to represent you.

How to find a lawyer

■ Call any lawyers you know for a recommendation.

■ If a friend or family member has used a lawyer for a car-related problem and been satisfied, ask that person for a recommendation.

■ Call the local bar association and ask for a recommendation.

■ Ask police officers or other court officials to recommend someone, since they're very familiar with lawyers in the community who handle these types of cases.

■ If you can get to a library, look in a directory of lawyers like Martindale-Hubbell. Or consult the online version of that directory at **www.martindale.com**. Use the "Lawyer Locator" feature and search by location and practice area. You can also search **www.findlaw.com**. Use the "Find Lawyers" function on the home page to search for criminal lawyers in your city and state.

Questions to ask when interviewing a lawyer

■ How much experience do you have with this type of case?

■ Have you practiced law in the community where my case is being brought? (If it's a criminal case, you want a lawyer who is familiar with the prosecutors and judges and has worked with them in the past.)

■ How long will my case take? Will I have to be at every court date?

■ What are your fees? Do I have to pay you a retainer—a payment before you begin working on the case? Or pay it all when the case is decided?

In a criminal case, you'd also want to ask about possible defenses to the charge and your chances of avoiding a conviction.

car accidents

When to hire a lawyer

Auto accidents are so common that even when you follow all the rules of the road, there's a chance you'll be involved in one at some point. From a minor fender bender to a more serious crash, it's a good idea to know what to do after an accident occurs—both as a good citizen and to protect yourself legally.

Most accident cases are resolved between the insurance company and the person making a claim to be compensated. But if you're injured, you'll generally be better served by having an attorney represent you from the beginning, unless it's a very minor injury. As you decide whether you need a lawyer, keep these thoughts in mind.

If you are bringing the case, there's little to lose in hiring a lawyer since accident lawyers typically take cases on a **contingency basis** (you will only pay attorney fees if you win your case, and the fees come out of the amount you recover). Always see a lawyer if there are serious injuries or considerable damages involved.

If you are the one being sued and you're concerned that the damages suffered by someone else are greater than your insurance policy covers, you should talk to a lawyer to determine whether you'll need personal representation in addition to the representation your insurer provides. Keep in mind that as a defendant, you'll be paying your own bills if you retain a lawyer.

One benefit of hiring a lawyer is that the facts in an accident are often not what they appear to be, and an experienced lawyer will be able to uncover information that helps your case. Also, if speeding and alcohol use (by you!) are involved, you'll certainly want to get a lawyer immediately (see page 84).

Make a photocopy of this list and leave it in your glove compartment.

Accident checklist

Stop your car. If you hit someone and leave the scene, you've committed a crime (which can result in losing your license, getting fined, and even going to jail). And since fault is not always easy to determine, you should stop even if you're not sure you were at fault. There is one exception: If you're on a deserted road and hit from behind, you should travel to the nearest well-lit place where you feel safe. It's possible that someone may hit you to get you out of your car so they can rob you.

1 If anyone is injured, call the paramedics. Don't try to provide help on your own unless you have training and know what you're doing.

2 Call the police to file a report if there's anything more than minor damage to anyone's car or if injuries are involved. It's a good idea to get the name and badge number of the officer because it may be easier to get a copy of the accident report with this information.

3 Exchange the following information with the other driver: names; phone numbers; insurance details; car registration information; makes, models, and years of cars; and license plate numbers. If you hit a parked car, leave this information on the windshield of the car you hit.

4 Find out who is the legal and registered owner of the other car (note—that may not be the same person as the driver).

5 Get the names and contact information for passengers in the other car, as they may be necessary as witnesses. Also try to get any witnesses who weren't in either car to stay until the police get there—or at least get their contact information.

6 While it's fresh in your memory, take notes about what happened and try to draw a diagram of the accident scene. Include any observations about the weather and road conditions, note the time of day, and try to estimate your speed and that of the other driver. Try to capture any details that may be relevant to someone's driving (e.g., if the driver was using a cell phone at the time of the accident).

7 Other than finding out if everyone is okay, avoid small talk with other drivers or passengers. Even if you think the accident was your fault, there are many facts that you may not know yet (e.g., the other driver was drunk, a traffic light was broken) and admissions at the scene of the accident could harm your legal position later on.

8 Do not tell anyone at the scene that you're not hurt unless you are sure, since it often takes a few days for injuries to surface.

9 Call your insurance company and report the accident.

accidents and insurance

Who pays for damages

In every accident, the issue of who is at fault is an important one since it determines who will ultimately pay for the costs associated with the accident.

Generally, the cost of repairing damage to a car and the medical costs of anyone injured will be paid by the person who caused the accident. This is why it's essential to have insurance. In fact, in most states you can't own a car without getting auto insurance, which covers a lot of the costs associated with accidents. For this protection, you pay a **premium**, a periodic payment to the insurance company. If you have a good driving record, your premium should stay roughly the same each year (although the insurance company is free to raise its rates). If you're at fault in an accident and a claim is brought against you, your premium may go up because you will be considered riskier to insure.

If you or the other person doesn't have insurance, things are a bit more complicated. If you have insurance and the other person doesn't, your insurance company may cover your expenses (especially if your policy includes "personal injury protection" and "uninsured" or "underinsured" motorist coverage).

You can also sue the other driver personally, but if the driver was not responsible enough to have insurance, he may not have any assets or income either, so you could be wasting your time. If you're at fault and you are uninsured, be prepared to be sued personally and be held legally responsible for the damages sustained by the injured parties.

I got hurt in an accident and the other driver's insurance company contacted me with an offer that seems fair. Is there any reason not to accept it then?

You should be wary about a quick offer from an insurance company. While you may be able to determine property damage soon after an accident, you may not know the costs of any personal injuries. If you've gotten an offer for a settlement so quickly, think about talking to a lawyer who can advise whether it's fair.

What if I lent my car to a friend and she caused an accident? Will my insurance cover it?

Probably, as long as the driver is using the car with your permission and is not excluded from your policy's coverage. Even if the damages exceed the policy limits, you probably won't be personally responsible for them unless you were negligent (e.g., you lent the car to someone with a terrible driving record).

What should I do if another driver caused an accident and says, "Let's not advise our insurance companies. I'll just take care of your damages."

Get the insurance information before you agree to anything. And be careful. Many people don't follow up on their offers. And even if someone was well-intentioned, the person could withdraw the offer if you develop serious injuries later on.

Are there times when I wouldn't want to notify my insurance company of an accident?

If you believe the damage to both cars is less than the amount of your **deductible** (the amount you must pay before your insurance company pays the rest of the bill), you and the other person may agree not to report the accident. But it can be difficult to estimate the cost of repairs or know whether any injuries will develop.

drunk driving

Long-term implications

Driving after a few drinks and getting caught is often the only brush with the criminal system that many people have. But it's serious business, as anyone who has been in a car accident involving alcohol use will tell you.

While the phrase "drunk driving" is commonly used, the legal standard is really whether a driver's ability to operate a vehicle has been diminished by alcohol—often called Driving Under the Influence (DUI) or Driving While Intoxicated (DWI). So what does that mean for you if you happen to be behind the wheel after a lapse in judgment or a drinking spree?

Typically, if an officer suspects you're drunk (usually after he observes erratic driving), he will pull you over, ask for your license and registration, and look around in your car—all the while making observations about your behavior. (Keep in mind that in most locations, erratic or unsafe driving is not required for a conviction.)

He may then ask you to step out of the car and per- form some tests to gauge your coordination and mental sharpness. There are several other types of tests that measure blood-alcohol levels, many of which occur where you are stopped or back at the police station, where you can expect to be taken if the officer doesn't like what he sees (see page 118 for an explanation of the arrest process). These can involve taking samples of your blood, breath, and urine. Depending on where you live, you may or may not be able to talk to an attorney before sub- mitting to a test. Even in states where you have the right to refuse these tests, you may be arrested for doing so. (Your license may be suspended, too.) And if your case ultimately goes to trial, the fact that you refused a test could bias a jury against you.

ASK THE EXPERTS

What are the possible penalties if I'm found guilty?

The penalties for drunk driving can be very stiff and have long-term effects. Depending on the severity of the case (and whether it's your first offense), you can be fined, lose your license, be put on probation, assigned to a rehabilitation program, or sentenced to jail time. You can also expect a drunk driving conviction to result in an increase in your insurance premiums. In a state that doesn't require insurance, you may find that no insurance company will cover you.

Will I need to hire a lawyer?

Unless you were undeniably drunk and are willing to plead guilty and accept whatever punishment law enforcement is seeking, you will probably want to be represented by a lawyer—and one with experience handling drunk driving cases. Having a lawyer will greatly improve your ability to keep your license, keep fees down, or minimize whatever penalties are sought against you.

Are there any defenses to a drunk driving charge?

The two basic defenses are some variety of "I wasn't driving" or "I wasn't drunk." Other defenses have to do with how the law is defined by a particular state. For example, in some states, driving a tractor while drunk may not be ground for conviction since a tractor would not fit the legal definition of a motor vehicle. This type of hairsplitting is where a lawyer comes in handy.

Do lawyers generally prefer to plea-bargain or go to trial in a drunk driving case?

It all depends on the case. When there are facts in the defendant's favor (e.g., the drinking was not extreme, no one was injured, or it was a first offense), lawyers often find that juries can be sympathetic, and therefore they recommend going to trial rather than settling a case.

speeding and moving violations

If you get pulled over

Other behaviors associated with driving that can get you into some legal trouble are speeding, running a red light, or missing a stop sign. You will probably not need to hire a lawyer if you're charged with speeding or a minor moving violation.

If you've been driving at a speed greater than the posted speed limit, you're unlikely to be arrested unless you have committed some other offense as well (like running a red light).

When you receive a traffic ticket, you generally have several options. You can pay the fine and accept the black mark on your driving record, or you can contest the ticket in court. Sometimes you may also have the option of paying the fine and attending traffic school, which can keep your driving record untarnished.

How you should respond to a speeding ticket depends on how serious the charge is. In many cases (especially if it's a first offense and you weren't going too fast), you can just pay the fine and be done with it. But speeding tickets often result in **points**—negative notations on your license to indicate driving infractions, according to a system run by your state's Department of Motor Vehicles.

If you receive a certain number of points on your license, it will be suspended. (Your state's Department of Motor Vehicles can tell you how many points.) So if you already have several points on your license and are in danger of losing it, you should talk to a lawyer to see if there's a way to challenge the ticket. Before you call a lawyer, you should call your insurance company to find out whether the ticket will increase your insurance premiums.

ASK THE EXPERTS

What are the potential penalties for a speeding violation?

While you're probably not going to be sent to jail (particularly for a first offense), speeding can have serious ramifications including fines (which could be as high as $300), having your license revoked, being required to attend traffic school, and increases in your insurance premiums. Often attending traffic school (which generally takes 6 to 8 hours) will clear your record, though some states have limits on how many times you can attend in a given time period.

What should I do if I'm stopped for speeding?

Rule #1—be polite and cooperative. Rule #2—be polite and cooperative. Often the officer hasn't yet made up his mind about giving you a ticket, and if you're rude, you could send him over the edge pretty quickly. Also make sure to have your license and registration handy.

Are there any defenses to speeding?

There are several defenses to speeding. If you're certain that you were not speeding, it's possible that the radar or other detector has malfunctioned. It's also possible that the officer was improperly trained on the equipment or made a mistake. Even if you admit that you were speeding, you can ask to be excused from the behavior due to extreme circumstances (e.g., there was a medical emergency). If you claim you have a medical excuse, be prepared to prove that it's valid.

traffic court

If you decide to fight a ticket you received for speeding, making an illegal U-turn, or some other moving violation, you would do so in traffic court. The reasons you might choose this route are that you didn't actually do anything wrong (e.g., the officer wrote down the wrong license plate number), or that, you have a good excuse for the violation (e.g., you were driving your pregnant wife to the hospital).

Claiming that you were unaware of the law (for instance, you didn't know the speed limit), that your violation didn't cause any harm, or telling a long elaborate tale to the judge about why you were speeding, generally will not get you off the hook.

In most cases, you don't need a lawyer to represent you in traffic court—you can plead your case on your own. But if you're at risk of losing your license because you have multiple points from previous traffic violations, it may be worth hiring a lawyer to help defend you.

If the officer doesn't show up in court

If the police officer who issued the ticket doesn't appear on your court date, there's a good chance your ticket will be dismissed. (In some cases, the judge might set a second court date, then dismiss the case if the officer doesn't show up a second time.) Even if you don't have a strong defense, it may be worth fighting a ticket for a minor violation on the chance that the police officer won't appear. That's more likely to happen if you were ticketed for going slightly above the speed limit than if you were going 40 miles per hour above the speed limit and ran a red light.

Strategies for fighting a traffic ticket

Learn the law you're charged with violating As with anything involving the law, the rules regarding traffic violations are more complicated than they might appear—and the officer who wrote your ticket may be unaware of all the details. Find the exact wording of the statute to see if there's a loophole that can help you. (You can search the state law section at **www.findlaw.com**.)

Ask for the officer's notes In many states, you have the right to see any notes the officer made after writing your ticket. Send a written request to the police agency that ticketed you and the agency prosecuting you. If you don't hear back, call the court clerk and ask how to submit a request to the judge asking her to order the notes released to you.

Challenge the officer's version of events Despite the fact that most judges are likely to believe a police officer, if you have witnesses that can back up your side of the story, you may be able to show that the light was still yellow, not red. A diagram of the street layout, position of cars, etc., can also illustrate that the officer didn't have a clear view of what happened.

Demonstrate you made a reasonable error If a stop sign was blocked by a tree branch, taking a photo of the scene can help illustrate why you missed it.

Prove your conduct was justified or necessary If you changed lanes over a double yellow line to avoid being hit by another car, or were speeding because of a real medical emergency to get to a hospital, the judge may view your violation as justified.

car problems

The lemon law can help

Picture this. You drive out of the dealership in your spanking new car, smelling that wonderful new-car smell. The interior is free from dog hair, coffee spills, and sand. The engine hums quietly. But what if your dream is soon shattered when you hear a grating noise. Do you have any recourse? Actually, there is help available—in the form of your car's warranty and a friendly little collection of laws commonly called the **lemon law**.

Think of the lemon law as a money-back guarantee on your car. This is how it works: If you buy or lease a car that turns out to have a defect that persists despite several attempts to repair it, the manufacturer is required to buy the car back from you or exchange it for a new one. Of course, there are a few catches. Cars are not taken back for minor problems and those that are easily repaired. But if your car has a serious defect that persists despite several repair efforts, you may be able to get yourself a replacement and recover any extra costs you incurred.

Keep in mind that your rights will vary from state to state. (See **www.lemonlawamerica.com** for links to state lemon law statutes.)

FIRST PERSON DISASTER STORY

Car problems were just the beginning

When I bought a new car last year, I had nothing but problems from the day I drove it home. I kept taking it back to the dealer to get various problems fixed, but other strange noises kept occuring during my morning commute. A friend at work told me about lemon law protection, so I called a lawyer and asked him to look into it, which ended up creating a whole other problem. My lawyer did get the car replaced, but it cost me a fortune in legal fees, and I later learned I could have filed a claim on my own! I should've done more research—and paid more attention to the fine print in the contract I signed with my lawyer! —Gina M.

If I can handle a lemon law complaint on my own, why should I use a lawyer?

This depends on where you live, which manufacturer you're dealing with, and whether your dealership is helpful (remember, someone you are suing is not always going to be friendly!). Lawyers with experience in this area will know the ins and outs of dealing with different manufacturers. In some states, your attorney's fees will be paid for you if you win. (In other states you may be responsible for the manufacturer's legal fees if you lose.) Whatever you do, save all your records and your receipts, because the burden will be on you to prove that you made the proper attempts to have the car repaired and that you complied with all relevant time limits.

How do I know whether the problem with my car is enough to consider it a lemon?

If your car has a condition that deprives you of some important aspect of its use, value, or your safety, then you might have a claim. Often, if you have made four or more repair attempts for the same defect within the warranty period, you'll qualify.

I leased my car and didn't start the lemon law claim process until near the end of my lease. Now I've already given my car back to the dealer. Is it too late to pursue my claim?

This is a bit like trying to return the sesame seeds on a bagel after you've already eaten it. You have significantly weakened your case by waiting for the lease to expire. After all, if you waited so long, it is arguable that the problem didn't interfere with your use of the car. That said, if the problem and your repair efforts began within the warranty period, you may have a claim and be entitled to a full refund.

now what do I do?

Answers to common questions

Do I have any recourse if I bought a used car from an ad in the paper and it turned out to be a dud?

If you bought your car from a dealer, you're probably in a better position than if you bought from a private individual "as is." First, many used cars are sold with a manufacturer's warranty (either time left on the warranty that comes with a new car or an extended warranty). When there's a warranty, the manufacturer has an obligation to honor it even with a new owner. If there's no warranty but the seller made claims about the car's condition that turned out to be false, you can sue the seller for fraud.

What if I thought I was fine immediately after an accident and developed a severe pain in my neck several months later?

It's always a good idea to go to your doctor soon after an accident if you think there's any chance you were injured. If you wait and then develop pain after you've settled a personal-injury claim with the insurance company or the driver, you will likely have lost the ability to sue.

What if I caused an accident because another car hit me, causing me to hit the car where an injury ultimately occurred?

First, make sure that the chain reaction scenario is reflected in the police report and in the information you provide to your insurer. It would be good to have a witness—or if possible, an admission from the driver of the car that hit you. If you didn't do anything that contributed to the accident, the driver that hit you is likely to be the one held responsible for it all.

I learned that the driver of the car that hit me was driving without a license and doesn't have any insurance. Is there any reason to sue him? What about criminal charges?

File a detailed police report so the authorities can take whatever action is appropriate. Once it's reported to the police, he may end up being prosecuted criminally. The police report will also be helpful for your insurance claim, if your policy covers accidents with an uninsured or underinsured driver. As for suing him personally, anyone who doesn't have insurance probably doesn't have much money either, so you may be wasting your time. If you can't find a lawyer willing to represent you, that's a good indication that the chances of recovery are quite slim.

now where do I go?!

CONTACTS

www.lemonlaw.com— site of law firm Kimmel & Silverman, which contains useful information for consumers who have purchased "lemons."

www.lemonlawamerica.com—learn about the lemon laws in your state and find a lawyer.

www.freeadvice.com—offers an extensive question and answer section on drunk driving (under "Criminal Law" header).

Driver Performance Institute **www.dui.com**—information on driving under the influence.

Car Accident Attorney Center **www.car-accidents.com**—features information about car accidents, including statistics, legal rights, and links to accident-injury lawyers around the country.

www.nolo.com—the "Traffic Tickets" section includes several useful articles on speeding tickets and traffic court.

National Highway Traffic Safety Administration **www.nhtsa.dot.gov**—lists information about warranties for problems with certain car models.

BOOKS

How To Settle Your Own Auto Accident Claim Without a Lawyer
by Benji O. Anosike

Beat Your Ticket: Go to Court & Win!
by David Brown

An Educated Guide to Speeding Tickets: How to Beat and Avoid Them
by Richard Wallace

CHAPTER 5

Personal-Injury Law

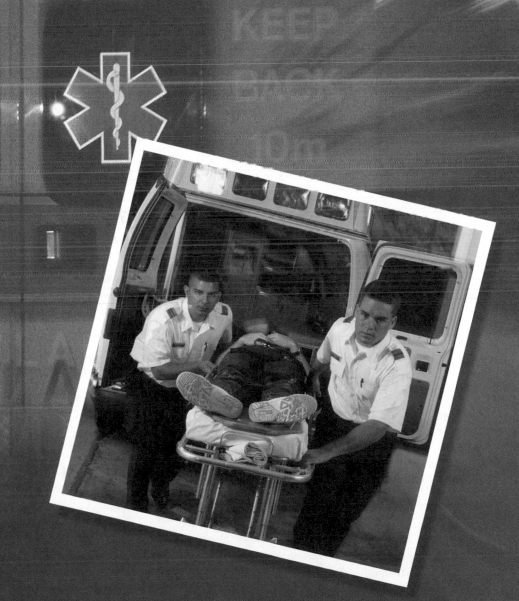

what is personal-injury law?

Hiring a personal-injury lawyer

Accidents happen. That's just a fact of life. But sometimes an accident has legal implications. Say you visit a doctor who mistreats your illness. Perhaps you use a household product that malfunctions and injures you. Or maybe you slip, fall, and break your leg at a restaurant where the floor was in need of repairs. And of course, you could be involved in a car accident (see pages 80–81 in addition to this chapter).

In any of these situations, if you believe that someone else's actions (or inactions) caused you injury, you might consider seeing a lawyer who can help figure out whether someone else was legally responsible for your injury, and if so, whether it makes sense to try to hold that person accountable.

This field of law has two sides: plaintiff and defense, referring to the two parties in a civil lawsuit. **Plaintiffs' lawyers** (also commonly referred to as trial lawyers) represent people who have been injured. **Defense lawyers** (who are usually retained by and paid by the defendant's insurance company) represent those accused of causing an injury. So in most cases you'll be looking for a lawyer who represents plaintiffs.

How to find a personal-injury lawyer

It's always a good idea to get a personal referral from someone you know who has used a personal-injury lawyer and had a good experience. You can also find listings of personal-injury lawyers through your state's trial lawyers association. To find the association in your state, contact the Association of Trial Lawyers of America at 800-424-2725 or on the Web at **www.atlanet.org** .

Other Internet resources to try include general search engines like Google and Yahoo!, or more specialized legal directories like Martindale-Hubbell (**www.martindale.com**) and Findlaw (**www.findlaw.com**). As you look through the directories, you'll notice that lawyers specialize by the type of injury, and some only take cases involving a certain disease or harmful substance (e.g., asbestos, tobacco-related cancer, lead contamination).

Questions for a Personal-injury Lawyer

How will you decide whether my case is worth accepting?
Your lawyer will consider factors such as whether you have suffered an injury that someone else is responsible for, whether it will be possible to prove that responsibility, and whether you've suffered damages as a result of the injury. Even if all of these factors point to taking the case, there must also be a way to collect damages from the person or entity responsible for your injury. (If there is no person or entity against whom you could collect a judgment, even the most aggressive lawyer would likely turn down your case.)

How do you charge?
Most lawyers bill clients by the hour, but personal-injury lawyers commonly charge a **contingency fee**—which means they get paid only if they win your case. (The fee comes out of the money received in a settlement.) The average contingency fee is between 25% and 40% of the money eventually recovered. Lawyers tend to take higher percentages for more complicated cases. Be wary of lawyers who charge a contingency fee and also request a **retainer**, up-front money to cover a portion of their expenses. It's rare for a client to be charged for expenses before the case is finished. Though practice varies depending on state law, if you lose your case, you may still have to pay your lawyer for expenses such as hiring experts or court filing fees. Make sure you understand what costs you'll be responsible for before signing a contract with the lawyer you hire.

the vocabulary of personal-injury law

As you enter the world of personal-injury law, there are a few important concepts and terms you should know:

One of the biggest concepts is called the **statute of limitations**, which is a requirement that a case be brought within a certain time period. Statutes of limitations vary by state as well as by **cause of action** (the legal theory, such as negligence or breach of contract, used to bring a case), but they're not negotiable. So if you've been injured and wait too long to see a lawyer about it, you may have lost the opportunity to sue.

When an accident happens, often there's a cause, and often the cause is that someone did something careless—or failed to do something, and that failure constituted careless behavior.

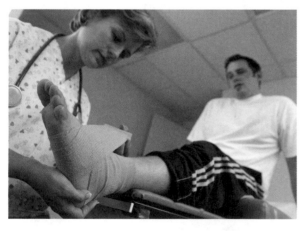

Negligence is a legal term that is used to describe such carelessness. Often the standard is that you must act as would a reasonably prudent person in the same or similar circumstances. For example, suppose there's a person who has a duty to behave in a careful manner, but that person does something careless that causes injury to another, and that injury causes the other party to incur damages. If all these elements are present, the careless person would be considered legally negligent.

Damages is the blanket term for all the ways a person has been harmed from an injury for which the law allows compensation. Some aspects are easy to calculate, such as lost wages from missed days at work or medical expenses. But it also includes intangibles like physical impairment, disfigurement, pain and suffering experienced after an injury. Damages are quite important in personal-injury cases because lawyers only take cases where they determine there are damages that can be recovered.

ASK THE EXPERTS

If many lawyers reject my case, what does it mean?

It probably means you don't have a good case, or that you have a good case but no likelihood of meaningful recovery—either because the damages are too small or because the defendant can't pay or lacks insurance. When lawyers work on a contingency basis, they only get paid if they succeed in getting a judgment that is recovered. So if the amount is likely to be very small, even if you've been injured and someone is clearly responsible for it, the lawyer's percentage may not be high enough to justify the time and expense it would take to handle the case.

What if I was injured and I've filed a claim with my insurance company to cover my medical expenses? Can I still file a lawsuit?

You certainly can, and many people pursue both avenues at once. From the beginning, your insurance may cover your medical expenses, but if you've incurred other costs like lost wages from time you missed at work, you'll want to try to recover those as well. A lawsuit can also help you recover future medical expenses and compensate you for damages like pain and suffering, which are hard to put a price on. Keep in mind that if your insurance company covers your medical expenses and you also collect a judgment in a lawsuit, the insurance company may try to get its hands on the amount that it had already paid. Personal-injury lawyers are quite familiar with managing such claims from insurance companies and should work to negotiate the best result on your behalf.

product liability

How to tell if you have a case

If you're using a product and that product injures you, you might wonder if the product is defective. The company that manufactured, sold, or distributed it may be responsible for your injuries. Holding the manufacturer responsible for defective products is what **product liability law** is all about.

But before you rush to sue, think about these questions that a personal-injury lawyer is likely to consider:

- Are the injuries suffered severe enough to warrant a lawsuit (e.g., can damages like medical expenses be proven that are high enough to justify taking the case)?

- Was the product being used according to its instructions or in a way that was foreseeable to the manufacturer?

- Did the manufacturer issue any warnings about a defect in the product? And if so, were you aware of those warnings?

- Did the manufacturer issue a product recall? (See box, next page.)

- If a suit is worth bringing, which parties should be sued? (The vendor, the manufacturer, the distributor, or any other entity in the chain of distribution can be sued in a case, since it's often unclear where the liability lies.)

- Is the defective product available as evidence? Your lawyer will want to see what the product looked like at the time it malfunctioned. If you alter it, you're tampering with an important piece of evidence in your case.

Many of these issues go to questions of **proof**—whether a lawyer will be able to prove that (1) your injuries exist, and (2) your injuries were caused by a defect in the product. Because these cases are often against big corporations who will likely retain top legal talent to defend lawsuits, product liability cases are very complex and require attorneys who are specialists with sufficient resources to compete with the big guns.

My husband died from taking his diabetes medicine. Can I sue on his behalf?

In most states, the representative of the estate of a person who dies can sue on behalf of that person's heirs and estate for damages suffered by that person until his death, as well as for the suffering of loved ones because of his death. In addition, parents, spouses, and children in many states have a claim for the loss of companionship and other things associated with the relationship. Remember, you'll need to get to a lawyer quickly because of the **statute of limitations**, which specifies the time period allowed for bringing the case.

What can I expect to collect in damages?

There are economic damages that are easily measured (e.g., lost wages, medical expenses) and noneconomic damages that are very difficult to calculate (e.g., pain and suffering, mental anguish. The exact amount of both will be determined by a judge or jury in a trial or in the process of a negotiation with the other side. The more seriously someone is injured, the greater the expectation that the damages would be higher.

What if I was partially at fault or was doing something I knew was dangerous when I was injured? Will that affect my case?

It very well may. The importance of a plaintiff's own responsibility for an injury varies from state to state. Your chances of recovery are certainly better if you were not doing something careless at the time, but depending on the standard in your state and the facts of your situation, you may still have a viable case.

Product recalls

When manufacturers realize that a product is defective, they may voluntarily or as a result of government intervention decide to recall that product.

Companies employ various methods of communicating a recall to consumers, including sending letters to warranty-holders and placing advertisements on television and radio stations. They do this for two reasons: (1) to protect consumers from getting injured, and (2) to limit their liability if they're sued.

If a product in question has been the subject of a recall, that certainly will be relevant to assessing a case involving the product—but the existence of a recall will not necessarily relieve a company from liability.

malpractice

When professionals make mistakes

When medical doctors and other medical professionals are sued for acting in a manner that doesn't meet the standard of care expected of them, they are sued for **medical malpractice**.

If you think you've been injured or haven't received proper care from someone in the medical profession, what should you do?

First, ask yourself whether your injury or condition was actually caused by the treatment you received. An imperfect outcome does not necessarily constitute malpractice. Many diseases do not respond to treatment, many treatments have known and disclosed risks, and doctors can't perform miracles. Nonetheless, there are situations in which a doctor failed to do something she was supposed to do in a given situation or did something she shouldn't have done. These types of cases are the basis for a malpractice lawsuit.

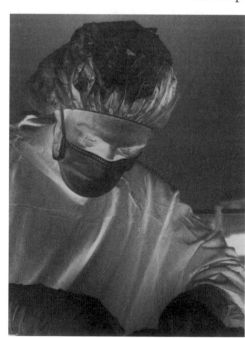

Medical malpractice can range from the obvious (e.g., a doctor operates on the wrong body part) to complications such as a patient's developing an infection after surgery.

Determining whether your doctor committed malpractice may not be clear to you, and it often requires getting a second opinion from another doctor (and even then, it may not be so clear). If you have your medical records, bring them with you to any doctor you see for a second opinion as well as to any lawyer you interview. If you don't have a copy of your records, ask your doctor for them. This is a routine patient request and you should not have difficulty obtaining them. Also, do your best to get the names of every medical professional who was involved in treating you, including nurses and physician's assistants.

ASK THE EXPERTS

I suspect my doctor made a mistake. Should I see a lawyer immediately?

Yes. A lawyer who specializes in medical malpractice will be able to help you figure out whether you have a case. There are strict laws regulating the timing of medical malpractice cases (and often requirements to have expert reports before a complaint can be filed). The laws vary by state, so be sure to consult someone knowledgeable about medical malpractice cases in your area.

Two weeks after a routine root canal, my recovery is not going well. I called the dentist and he told me to come right in. I don't trust him, so I don't want to go. What should I do?

Go to another dentist immediately. If you don't and your condition worsens, you may be partially to blame for your condition, and that fact may affect any case you may have had against your original dentist.

Before my surgery I signed a consent form. Will this prevent me from suing my doctor if something goes wrong?

Not necessarily. A consent form is a document advising a patient of the potential risks and complications of a procedure. When you sign such a form, you're considered to be notified about the information in the document (so be sure to read it first). Thus, if there was a risk of infection from your surgery and you contracted an infection (assuming the doctor performed the procedure according to the proper medical standards), you will probably have a weak case. On the other hand, if your doctor's treatment fell below the standard of care expected of physicians during such a procedure, you'll likely have a strong case whether or not you signed the form.

class-action lawsuits

How they work

When many people have been similarly injured or used the same defective product (see page 100), the cases of those people can be joined together in what's called a class action. Often, this happens when the injuries of each individual are too small to justify a lawyer's bringing an individual case. In such instances, you might notice advertisements on television or in newspapers alerting consumers about the lawsuit and how to take part in any financial recovery won by the lawsuit.

If a class-action case is successful, the result is often a large sum of money that is extremely tiny when divvied up among the thousands of consumers in the case. If you've been seriously injured, make sure to talk to a lawyer before joining a class action and/or to learn how to opt out of a class action that you may automatically be included in, as you may have a strong enough case to pursue on your own.

FIRST PERSON DISASTER STORY

Wasted time and nothing to show for it

I got a notice in the mail about getting involved in a class-action case involving a stock I purchased a few years ago. The notice contained complicated directions about what I needed to do if I wanted to participate, like providing records showing I bought the stock within the time period covered by the case. Finding those records in my attic and going to the post office to send them via certified mail took almost an entire day. In return, I later got a check for just $25! Next time, I'm going to read these things more carefully. If I knew what the financial recovery was going to be, I don't think I would have wasted all that time. —Irving M.

ASK THE EXPERTS

What should I do if I see an advertisement alerting people to a legal action involving a medical condition I have been suffering from?

When you see such an ad, it means that the law firm running the ad is involved in cases involving a certain type of injury. The first thing you should do is collect information. As a starting point, call the law firm and find out what the case is about. Ask exactly what injury, product, or practice is involved. Details will be very important. Then talk to your doctor to review your medical condition. You can also ask the law firms involved in these cases if there are doctors who are experts on the particular medical condition who may be available for consultation. Keep in mind that the law firm that placed that advertisement is probably not the only one representing people suffering from your illness. To find other law firms involved in a case, you can call the trial lawyers association or do a quick Internet search using the name of the injury, disease, or product as a key word.

If I think a product that injured me has injured other people as well, will I need to find a group to sue those responsible, or can I just worry about my own case?

If you find a lawyer willing to help you, she will figure out whether it makes sense to pursue the case on an individual basis or as a plaintiff in a class action. If it's the latter, it won't be your responsibility to assemble the other plaintiffs in the case—your lawyer will take care of that.

assault and battery

When you're
threatened or hurt

Consider the following scenarios: You were robbed and, in the course of the robbery, your attacker broke your nose; a physician inappropriately touched you or hurt you during an examination; your child was punished by a teacher with physical contact you consider excessive. All of these situations could involve cases of assault and/or battery against the person causing the harm described. Assault and battery are terms normally associated with criminal cases, but they can be causes of action in civil cases as well. An **assault** is an attempt by one person to physically harm another—it can be a mere threat and often doesn't involve physical contact. A **battery** is any intentional physical harm by one person to another.

In cases of assault and battery, the government usually brings criminal charges against alleged **perpetrators** (those suspected of inflicting the injuries upon a victim). The government prosecutes these cases, assigning and paying its own lawyers (usually called **district attorneys**) to bring it to trial. The victim is a material witness in the government's criminal case against the perpetrators.

In a criminal case, the victim may not be financially compensated. In such instances, the victim may wish to file a **civil** case against the perpetrators for assault and battery. That means the victim now becomes the plaintiff (the one bringing a lawsuit) and has to hire a lawyer, typically one who specializes in personal-injury law (see page 96). Often, a civil case for battery or assault is filed at the same time as a criminal case. Since the goal in a civil case is usually to recover monetary damages, your lawyer will want to establish two things—that you suffered damages as a result of your injuries, and that any financial judgment against the defendant will be collectible. To help your lawyer prove your damages, keep records of anything that relates to your injury (e.g., bills for medical treatment, physical therapy, or counseling) as well as any other ways you have been adversely affected (e.g., time lost from work).

My husband was injured by a drunk driver who was convicted after a criminal case. The driver was sentenced to 5 years in prison, but my husband can no longer work. Can we use a civil case to recover something to compensate our family for the loss of my husband's wages?

Yes. You can file a civil case against the drunk driver. Even though someone is in prison, if you get a judgment, he'll be responsible for paying it, assuming he has any assets or insurance. Bear in mind that even if he wasn't convicted in the criminal case, you could file a civil case against him (and the fact that he wasn't convicted won't necessarily affect his liability in a civil case because the evidence required for civil liability is less than what is required for a criminal conviction).

What if the defendant in a civil case doesn't have money to cover a judgment?

Your lawyer will likely be very concerned about the financial situation of the defendant, particularly if the defendant is an individual. If the defendant doesn't have assets that would cover a damage award, it may be possible to look to a homeowner's or other insurance policy, garnish wages (collect the money directly from his employer), or find some other method of collecting a judgment. But at the end of the day, if a judgment is unlikely to be collected, it may not be worth your time (or that of your lawyer) to go forward with a case.

now what do I do?

Answers to common questions

I think I have a very strong case, but my lawyer seems to have lost interest in pursuing it. What can I do?

Lawyers can only move as quickly as the courts allow, so don't confuse a slow pace with laziness. But if you're not hearing from your lawyer, make sure to call him regularly to obtain a status report or ask him to keep you informed in writing monthly. If you're still dissatisfied, write your lawyer a letter of complaint. If all else fails, you may want to switch lawyers and report your lawyer's behavior to the local bar association. Even the threat of doing so may spark some activity from your lawyer. Keep in mind that finding a lawyer to take a case already under way can be difficult, so before you fire one, have another one lined up who is willing to represent you. If you replace your lawyer, make sure to get a written release from the first attorney or you could end up owing both.

I lost my case the first time around. Can I take another stab?

You don't necessarily get to try again simply because you don't like the outcome of your case. Challenging a verdict is called an **appeal**. Whether a case can be appealed is a very technical question, and the standards for bringing an appeal are quite high. For example, if the judge made a significant error that affected the outcome of the case, there may be grounds for appeal. On the other hand, if you have learned some new facts about the situation that caused your injury, you will probably not be able to appeal the case. Appealing a case simply means you have a right to a new trial. Both the plaintiff and the defendant have the right to appeal a verdict as long as they satisfy the proper criteria.

Is there a value in settling my case before trial?

It depends. The jury you get may not be sympathetic to your case. And even if a jury is on your side, they still may disagree with you about the cash value attached to your pain. There is always some element of risk when a case goes to trial, because even the most seasoned lawyers can't predict the composition or the opinion of a jury. Another advantage to settling a case is that a settlement can't be appealed.

I've been injured, but I haven't been able to find a lawyer to take my case. I still want to pursue the matter. How can I convince someone to represent me?

If you have talked to several lawyers and no one will represent you, you probably don't have a strong case. Lawsuits are not always the answer. As you think about filing a lawsuit, ask yourself, "Is it really worth my time and emotional effort to go through the process of suing someone if I'm unlikely to accomplish anything?"

now where do I go?!

CONTACTS

www.consumerlawpage.com—sponsored by a law firm, a good site for general information.

www.findlaw.com—legal portal for legal professionals, students, the public, and businesses. In the "Public" section, look under "Injuries" for resources.

U.S. Consumer Product Safety Commission, **www.cpsc.gov**—the CPSC is the government agency charged with protecting the public from unsafe and defective products. It's a useful resource to get information about product hazards and recalls.
330 East-West Highway
Bethesda, MD 20814-4408.
301-504-0990, Fax 301-504-0124
and 301-504-0025.

BOOKS

The Law of Personal Injury
by Margaret Jasper

How to Win Your Personal Injury Claim
by Joseph L. Matthews

Law of Product Liability
by Margaret C. Jasper

Then Why Does It Still Hurt?
A Book About HMOs, Managed Care, Medical Malpractice and You
by Jack Schroder

Run-ins with the law

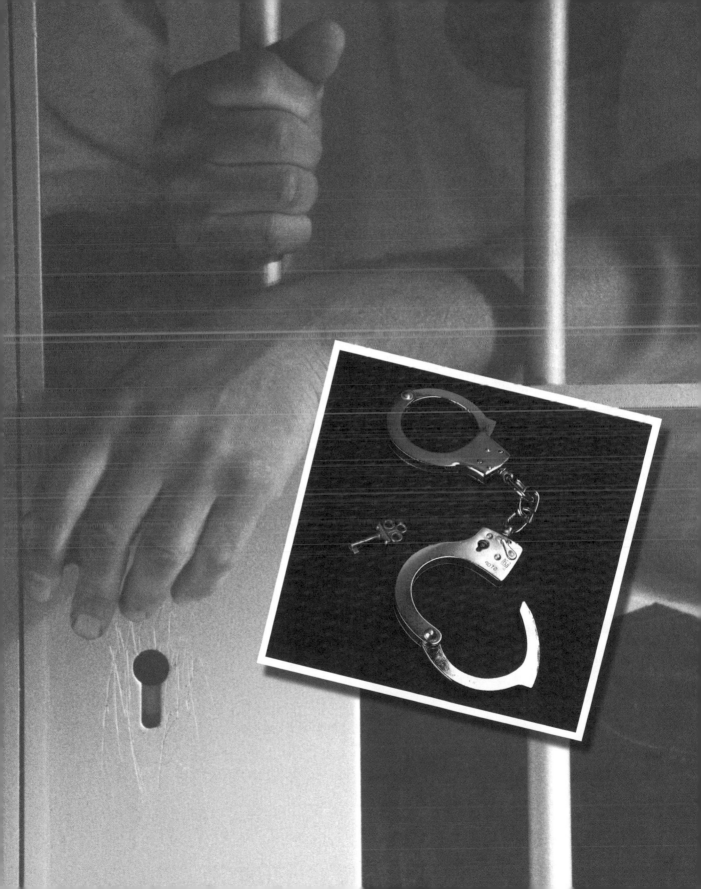

what is criminal law?

Legal terms defined

You answer a knock on your door to find a police officer standing outside with a warrant for your arrest. Or you're pulled over on the highway and the officer asks to search your car. Either of these scenarios, and many others, could be your introduction to the criminal justice system.

As you probably know from television and the movies, under the American legal system, the person accused of a crime (called the **defendant**) is entitled to a lawyer regardless of the type of crime.

Crimes fall into two major categories—**felonies** and misdemeanors. Each state has its own definitions, but you can gener-

ally think of felonies as major crimes like murder, rape, and drug trafficking. If you're convicted of a felony, you can expect to suffer a stiff penalty, probably including a jail sentence. Conviction for a felony can also result in the loss of certain civil rights, like the right to vote. **Misdemeanors** are less serious crimes like shoplifting and vandalism and are often punishable by a fine or a brief jail sentence.

Within the felony and misdemeanor categories, crimes are broken down into those against people (e.g., assault, battery, robbery), those against property (e.g., burglary, arson), those against the public (e.g., possession of drugs, prostitution), and those involving motor vehicles (see page 78).

How to find a lawyer

■ Call any lawyers you know for a recommendation (even if they don't do criminal work, they can probably help you find someone).

■ If a friend or family member has used a criminal lawyer in the past and has been satisfied, ask that person for a recommendation.

■ Call the bar association in your area or where you were charged with the crime.

■ Ask police officers or other court officials to recommend someone, since they're very familiar with lawyers in the community who handle criminal cases.

■ If you can get to a library, look in a directory of lawyers like Martindale-Hubbell. Or consult the online version of that directory at **www.martindale.com**. Use the "Lawyer Locator" feature and search by location and practice area. You can also search **www.findlaw.com**. Use the "Find Lawyers" function on the home page to search for criminal lawyers in your city and state.

Questions to ask when interviewing a lawyer

■ Do you focus exclusively on criminal law? (Criminal law is highly specialized, so you want someone who's an expert in your type of case.)

■ Have you practiced law in the community where my case is being brought? (You want a lawyer who's familiar with the prosecutors and judges and has worked with them in the past.)

■ What are the possible defenses to this crime? What are my chances of avoiding a conviction?

■ How long will my case take? Will I have to be at every court date?

■ What are your fees? Do I have to pay you a deposit up front? Or do I pay it all when the case is decided?

criminal lawyers

Lawyers who specialize in criminal defense

To avoid being intimidated by the drama of a criminal case, it helps to know who is doing what. In a criminal case, suits are brought by the government against individuals. **Prosecutors** (also called district attorneys, state's attorneys, and United States Attorneys) are attorneys who represent the government (also referred to as the People of the United States). Their role is to bring lawsuits on behalf of the government against defendants. **Defense attorneys** are lawyers who represent defendants.

If you're a defendant and can't afford to hire your own lawyer, you'll be appointed one by the court (these are called **court-appointed lawyers** or **public defenders**). If you can afford a lawyer, you can hire a **private lawyer** who specializes in criminal defense. The system for assigning public defenders varies from state to state (there can even be differences within a state), so there is no hard-and-fast rule about how much you can make and still qualify for representation by a public defender.

Between You and Your Lawyer

When dealing with criminal lawyers, it's important to know that you have a **privilege of confidentiality**, which means that your lawyer is not allowed to reveal anything you say to anyone else. But avoid speaking with your lawyer when you're in a public place; people who overhear your conversations are not bound to keep to themselves what you say.

ASK THE EXPERTS

What's the difference between a state offense and a federal offense? Is a federal offense necessarily more serious?

The difference depends on whether the charge involves a state or federal law. Every state has its own penal code, the body of laws enacted by the state legislature that defines what is considered "criminal" under that state's standards. In addition to those state laws, the U.S. Congress has enacted a separate framework of laws that are enforced by the federal government through its offices around the nation; crimes defined by those laws are called federal offenses. Often federal crimes involve a nationwide issue (e.g., drug trafficking).

Federal offenses are not necessarily more serious than state crimes, they are just different. For example, a conviction for carrying out a robbery across state lines could carry a lighter penalty than a conviction for murder under a state statute.

I've heard that I may be able to represent myself. Is that a good idea?

A defendant who represents himself in court is called a **pro se**. But veteran criminal lawyers generally consider self-representation misguided. Criminal law is very complex; your chances of obtaining the best outcome in your case improve greatly if you put yourself in the hands of an expert.

What do criminal lawyers charge?

Hourly rates will vary based on geography, complexity of the case, and experience of the lawyer. You may also be able to negotiate a flat fee for the entire case, which is advisable if it's complex. Be prepared to pay the majority of the cost up front. Also keep in mind that you'll be paying your lawyer whether you win or lose.

searches

When the police look for evidence

When the police suspect that a crime has been committed, they can obtain a **search warrant** to look for evidence of the crime in your car, your home, or any other place they think evidence may be located. To get a search warrant, the police need to go before a judge or **magistrate** (a person authorized by the court to issue warrants and conduct other court processes) and show **probable cause** (the reasons they believe a crime has been committed).

Sometimes, if the police are afraid that evidence will be destroyed or moved, they may be able to perform a search without taking the time to get a warrant. There are also other situations when a warrant is unnecessary, such as when evidence is in **plain view** (e.g., an officer pulls you over because you were swerving on the highway and sees a six-pack of beer next to you).

As with a search of your home or car, a police officer who suspects criminal activity may search your person in what is known as a **frisk** (a quick pat-down of your outer clothing). A frisk may be permitted without a warrant if a police officer has reason to believe that you may be armed or pose some other danger to the officer.

Strip searches, which are very rare and often illegal, may be done in certain circumstances, one of which is if an officer suspects that drugs or other contraband have been hidden in or on your person. Standard practice is that strip searches are conducted by officers of the same sex as the accused.

ASK THE EXPERTS

If I'm stopped in my car and a police officer without a warrant asks to search the car, do I have to let him?

You always have the right to refuse an officer's request to conduct a search. Keep in mind, however, that if you refuse, the police may be able to detain you for a "reasonable" period of time until they obtain a search warrant. There is no standard for what is reasonable—it will be determined based on the circumstances.

What if a friend is visiting me and, without telling me, brings something illegal into my home. Could I be held responsible?

It is generally not the intent of the law to punish unknowing conduct. So if a search turns up illegal evidence that doesn't belong to you and you didn't know it was in your home, you shouldn't be held responsible for your friend's criminal behavior. Nonetheless, you might initially be charged with a crime based on that evidence, in which case you would have to get a lawyer and defend yourself.

If the police show up at my house with a search warrant, can they search anywhere in the house without any limitations?

They can search anyplace the items named in the warrant might reasonably be found. For example, if the warrant is for guns and ammunition, the police could search even a small pill-box since it's possible that a bullet could be hidden within it. On the other hand, if the police are searching for a getaway car, they could look in your backyard but not in your bathtub.

The importance of search procedures

As you can see, there are many procedures that must be followed for a police search to be considered legal. If the proper procedures are followed and the police find damaging evidence during the search, whatever they find may be considered admissible during your case (which means it can be introduced at your trial to show that you're guilty).

If the police don't follow proper procedures, your lawyer may be able to convince the court that even if there is evidence that would be harmful to your case, it must be suppressed (which means that it can't be introduced against you at your trial).

arrest and booking

Being brought into police custody

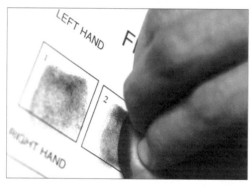

If the police want to arrest you, they generally need to get an **arrest warrant** by appearing before a judge or magistrate and presenting evidence that a crime has been committed and that you are a **suspect**—a person the police believe committed the crime. (In some instances, the police can make an arrest without a warrant, such as when they witness a crime being committed.)

After the police have obtained an arrest warrant, they'll find you and take you back to the police station (probably in handcuffs). Once you are brought into **custody** (which generally means you are in the police station, but could also be any other place from which you're not free to leave), the police must remind you of your rights before they can question you. Called **Miranda rights**, they protect you from unintentional self-incrimination (see box on opposite page).

After you're read your rights and indicate, sometimes with a signed statement, that you understand them, the police may begin questioning you, if you agree to talk with them. If you ask for a lawyer to be present during questioning, which is generally a good idea, the police must wait until the lawyer arrives before asking any further questions. See page 113 for tips on finding a criminal lawyer.

Booking Basics

At the station, the police will ask for information that confirms your identity, like your Social Security number, in a process called being **booked**. They'll also take your personal property and hold it while you're in custody, and you may be fingerprinted, photographed, or asked to submit to breath or blood tests. In certain jurisdictions, if you refuse to submit to tests such as a **breath alcohol test** (which measures the amount of alcohol in your system), the government may use your refusal as evidence of your guilt.

ASK THE EXPERTS

What if a friend of mine is being roughed up by the police while he is being arrested, and I intervene?

Expect to be arrested. You could be arrested for a number of charges including disorderly conduct, disturbing the peace, aiding an escape, or even as an accessory-after-the-fact to a crime. Your best approach may be to simply witness it and then report it later to the police department nearest the incident. If possible, get it on video or get other witnesses to see what's happening.

If a police officer presents me with a warrant for my arrest, do I have to go?

If the officer has a warrant, you must go. In fact, in some states even if the arrest is illegal or is based on an improperly obtained warrant, it may be a crime to resist the arrest.

Is it a good idea to talk to a lawyer before taking a breath test?

If you can talk to a lawyer first, you may be able to discreetly ask for advice on what to do. But be mindful that others may hear what you tell your lawyer, and they're not bound to keep it quiet.

Are there any times I wouldn't be read my rights?

Miranda warnings are only required when two things happen: you are in police custody, and the police are questioning you. If the police don't want to ask you questions, they don't need to recite the Miranda warnings; or if you volunteer information, Miranda may not apply. If you weren't read your Miranda rights, it doesn't mean the case will be dismissed; at most, statements you made without having been read the warnings will be suppressed at your trial.

Miranda rights

Going through the Miranda warnings has been a required part of police procedure since the decision in a 1966 Supreme Court case, *Miranda v. Arizona.* The warnings are:

- You have the right to remain silent. Should you give up the right to remain silent, anything you say may be used against you in a court of law.

- You have the right to an attorney and to have that attorney present during any questioning by the police. If you can't afford one, one will be appointed for you at no cost.

- If you choose to talk to the police, you have the right to stop the questioning at any time.

jail and bail

How to post bail

Between the time of arrest and a **first appearance** in court, when you're formally charged with a crime and allowed to plead guilty or not guilty, you may be waiting in a local jail or some other facility.

In order to be freed, you may be required to **post bail** (put up a sum of money) to ensure that you will appear in court. If you don't appear in court, you (or anyone who put up the money for you) will lose the amount of the bail, and a warrant for your arrest will be issued. At the end of a case, whether you're convicted or not, you will get the bail money back.

In setting the amount of bail, a judge looks at your prior criminal history, whether you've lived in the same community for a long time, the severity of the crime, whether you pose a danger to anyone if released from jail, and whether you're likely to flee before your trial. Some charges are so serious that the judge will decide to hold the defendant without bail until the case is over.

If you cannot get enough money together to make bail, some states allow you to **post a bond**, which is a way to raise the bail money without putting up the whole amount (sort of like a mortgage). To get a bond, you can go to a **bondsman**, who will pay the full bail amount to the court for you in exchange for a nonrefundable fee (usually about 10% of the bail amount). The bondsman may perform a credit check or require reference letters, and may refuse to lend you the money. It's typical for bondsmen to require you to secure the loan with property or other valuables in case you don't appear in court.

If you have no record, the offense is minor, or you can convince the judge that you're not a flight risk, you may be **released on your own recognizance** (also called O.R., or P.R. for personal recognizance). You can get out merely by promising to appear at the court date.

ASK THE EXPERTS

Will I be kept in jail a long time before getting the opportunity to post bail? Is it common to have to sleep in jail overnight?

In most states, you're brought to court the same day you're arrested; in others it could be the next business day. Bear in mind courts operate only on weekdays, so if you're arrested on a Friday night, you could spend the whole weekend in jail. Even if you have a private lawyer, you may not be able to avoid spending a night in jail.

What if I can't raise the money for bail or a bond?

You'll be held in some facility until your case is resolved. In most jurisdictions any time you spend in **pretrial detention** (in jail awaiting trial because you couldn't make bail) will be credited toward your sentence if you're ultimately required to serve jail time.

pleading

You have
several options

Your first opportunity to speak with the judge or have a lawyer speak for you usually takes place at the **arraignment**, when you're formally presented with charges against you and given the opportunity to **plead** in response to those charges (you admit or deny them).

In terms of pleading, you will always have one of two options, guilty or not guilty. Some states also allow you to plead **nolo contendere** (also called **no contest**).

A **guilty plea** is an admission to the court that you committed the crime. This can also come about during a **plea bargain** (a negotiated deal between the defense and the prosecution that resolves the case without a trial). This often includes pleading guilty to a less serious charge or agreeing to a lighter sentence. These deals occur in the vast majority of criminal cases.

If you plead guilty, you give up certain constitutional rights (generally the right to a trial, the right to confront witnesses against you, and the right against self-incrimination). If you plead guilty, the most common next step is sentencing, when the court determines your punishment.

A **not guilty plea** does not necessarily mean "I'm innocent." It's a way to say to the government, "Prove it." (See page 125 for an explanation of defenses).

Nolo contendere is complicated. It means that you are neither admitting nor denying the charges, but have decided not to contest the government's case against you. There will be no trial—a judge will impose the sentence. The main difference between this and a guilty plea is that you're not admitting guilt. The end result is often the same, however, so if nolo is permitted in your state, you will need to discuss with your lawyer the implications of pleading it.

ASK THE EXPERTS

How much time will there be between when I was arrested and the time I go to trial or enter a plea?

It varies greatly. As a defendant, time can can work in your favor. Crimes may seem less serious, witnesses or victims may become less interested in pursuing the case, or you may have participated in counseling or other recovery program that will improve a court's opinion of your case. Typically, when the defendant is in jail (as opposed to free on bail) a case will be tried or otherwise resolved more quickly.

What happens between the time of arrest and the time of trial?

Before the trial, many procedural steps take place, and the prosecuting attorney and your lawyer exchange certain required information (this process is called **discovery**). This is also the time that your attorney uses to prepare your defense, which includes interviewing you, investigating the charges, and locating witnesses. Your attorney should keep you informed of developments in your case.

Why would anyone plead guilty?

Some consideration is given to a person who admits that he has committed a crime, because it saves time and money in going to trial. Often, pleading guilty to a less serious crime will mean that a defendant can receive a more lenient sentence than may be imposed if the government wins at trial.

defense

Common defense strategies

Unless you plead guilty, the next step will be figuring out how to defend against the charges that have been made. Defenses to crimes generally fall into two broad categories: factors that **exculpate** (get you off the hook, so charges are dismissed or the verdict is not guilty) and those that **mitigate** (factors that can lessen the punishment or the seriousness of the charge even though you may be found to have committed a crime). Having a good defense does not mean you won't be charged with the crime, but it may mean that you are **acquitted** at trial (meaning the charges against you are dismissed).

The chart on the opposite page is just an overview of some basic defense principles and how they can have an impact on your case. Keep in mind that each of these defenses is very complex, and how they work varies from state to state.

These defenses can also play out differently depending on whether the offense involves **specific intent** to commit a crime (you knew what you were doing and you knew it was illegal) as opposed to a **general criminal intent** (you knew what you were doing, whether or not you knew it was illegal). Our criminal system is designed to punish those who commit an act intentionally. Therefore, information that shows you didn't intend to commit a crime may be helpful to your defense. This does not mean that ignorance of the law is a defense.

Common defenses and how they work

Defense	Explanation	Result
Consent of victim	This defense argues that the act was not a crime because the victim consented to it. It is often used in date-rape cases where the defendant claims the victim wanted to have sex but called it a rape after the fact. This defense can only be used if the victim is legally capable of consenting (e.g., she was over the age of majority and was sober at the time).	Exculpates
Self-defense, defense of another, defense of property	This argument claims you committed the crime in order to protect yourself, someone else, or your property. In order to succeed, the force used must not be greater than was reasonably necessary under the circumstances.	Exculpates
Intoxication	Intoxication is not necessarily a defense, but since it can affect your ability to reason, it may be raised to show you didn't intend to commit a certain crime. Obviously, drunkenness would not be a valid defense to a charge involving intoxication (see page 84).	Mitigates
Entrapment	If you can prove you were set up or coerced by the police to commit a crime that you wouldn't normally have committed, you may have a successful entrapment argument. This defense is most commonly used in crimes involving solicitation (e.g., drugs, prostitution, and certain Internet crimes).	Exculpates
Alibi	An alibi is used to show that you couldn't have committed a crime, because at the time it happened, you were somewhere else.	Exculpates
Insanity	This is an unusual defense—when successful, you are conceding that you committed the crime alleged, but because of a mental disorder you were unable to control your behavior and shouldn't be held responsible.	This may keep you out of jail, but it may not keep you out of a state-run facility for the criminally insane.

trial

In the vast majority of states, you have a right to be tried by a jury of your peers in all criminal cases. As a defendant, you have the right to decide if you'd prefer to be tried only in front of a judge. A judge-only trial is also called a **bench trial**. A good lawyer will be able to help you decide which to choose; it will generally depend on the strength of your case, who the judge is, and the specific details of your case.

If you're tried by a jury, both lawyers will have done a lot of work before the trial date. They will have made decisions on strategy (which witnesses to call, which facts to build their case around, etc.), and they may have filed **motions**, which are petitions asking the judge to decide on certain matters before the trial begins. Two of the most common motions your attorney may file are: (1) to challenge whether evidence seized by the police can be presented in court, or (2) to suppress statements made during police questioning.

A trial begins with **opening statements**, speeches by the opposing lawyers. First the prosecution and then the defense will preview the case and outline the issues to be presented. These statements are meant to be free from argument and merely a statement of the relevant facts; but in reality, deft attorneys use the opening statement to begin the task of persuasion.

In preparing the case, each side will be able to call **witnesses**, people they think will be helpful to their side of the case or harmful to the other side. Each side can ask questions of its witnesses (**direct examination**) and then the other side will have the opportunity to ask questions (**cross-examination**). This process begins with the prosecution's witnesses, and when the prosecution concludes (also called **resting its case**), the defense presents its case.

ASK THE EXPERTS

What if I know the prosecution is wrong about something? Can I interrupt?

No, that's why you hired a lawyer—it will be her job to make appropriate objections. When she does this, the judge will either accept the objection and tell the jury to disregard the improper testimony; or he will overrule it, which means that the testimony stands and is part of the trial record. If you can't control yourself, be aware that some states permit the court to order an unruly defendant to be removed from court or shackled and gagged during the proceedings.

Why are some prisoners allowed to wear street clothes and others made to wear their prison garb? Doesn't seeing you in your prison uniform bias the jurors?

It's definitely not a good idea to appear before the jury in the prison jumpsuit you will be in if you never made bail. Often criminal lawyers will get in touch with a defendant's family members to arrange for some presentable clothes for court appearances.

If I'm the defendant, do I have to testify as a witness in the case?

The U.S. Constitution gives defendants in criminal cases the right to be free from **self-incrimination**. In all criminal cases, the prosecution has the burden of proving the case, and the defendant can't be forced to testify in his own trial. This means that you can choose to remain silent while the government puts on its case. This is an important decision, which you should discuss with your lawyer. For example, say you were previously convicted of a crime. If you decided to testify, the prosecuting attorney might be allowed to question you about the previous conviction, which could affect the jury's opinion of you.

sentencing

What's the penalty?

At the end of the trial, after hearing all the evidence, the judge or jury will determine the verdict. There are three possible outcomes—**acquittal** (not guilty), guilty of the offense charged, or **guilty of a lesser-included charge** (a less serious crime). In a jury trial, most states require that every member of the jury agree to **convict** (find guilty) or **acquit** (find not guilty). If the jury cannot agree unanimously, then it is called a **hung jury**, and the case may have to be retried (a decision that's up to the government). If there is no retrial, that's good news for you. Except in rare instances, the case is over and you are free.

If a guilty verdict is returned, **sentencing** begins (determining what the penalty will be). It can be done by either the judge or the jury, depending on your state's laws, and it may be part of the trial or handled in a separate proceeding.

The three goals of criminal sentencing are **rehabilitation** (which seeks to educate or reform a person convicted of a crime), **deterrence** (which seeks to prevent people from committing the same crime again), and **punishment** (meting out some penalty considered appropriate to the crime.)

Rehabilitation is usually attempted through periods of **probation**, when the offender's conduct is monitored through regular meetings with a court officer. Probation generally has conditions attached to it— performing community service, obtaining counseling, or attending substance-abuse programs to address the underlying causes of the criminal conduct. A judge may impose probation in place of or in addition to prison time.

The most common sentences are monetary fines, probation, and jail, or a combination of all three. The severity of the sentence is based on the facts of the case, the impact of the crime, and the offender's prior criminal record.

What happens after the trial?

Even if you're in prison, you still have rights under our criminal justice system, and the legal process can continue if you feel you were wrongly convicted. You may file an **appeal**, a process by which a court can overturn a guilty verdict. Appeals allow you to challenge the interpretation of the law but not challenge factual issues like how fast you were driving. Although many prisoners mount their own appeals and use their time in prison to study the record of their case, the success rate for appeals is much higher when handled by lawyers.

How long will a conviction stay on my record?

Except in some cases involving minors, convictions stay on your record unless you apply to get your record **expunged**, which means it is sealed and will not be accessible to anyone outside the criminal justice system. Getting your record expunged is difficult, and the procedures to do it vary from state to state. If this is something you're interested in, you should talk to a lawyer about whether your conviction is one that can be expunged and what is involved in your state.

If I'm sentenced to a prison term, will I have to serve the entire sentence?

In almost all jurisdictions, you can do things to earn credits to reduce your sentence (e.g., taking high school or college courses, completing a substance-abuse program). It depends on how motivated you are and how many programs are available in your state or in that prison. If you earn such credits, you may be let out early on **parole**, which means you've been released from prison but will have to abide by certain rules upon your release. Failure to do so will land you back in prison.

victims' rights

Help for crime victims

If you're the victim of a crime, you have most likely experienced some kind of trauma and may need help in the healing process. Unfortunately, many victims don't feel this happens during a criminal case. This is because the prosecuting attorney doesn't represent the victim, he represents the citizens of the United States (also called **the People** or **the State**). His ethical obligation is to seek justice, not to zealously represent the victim.

Over the years, advocates have argued for the improvement of programs to aid victims. As a result, most states have adopted a "victim's bill of rights," which outlines the various rights afforded to victims of crimes. At the least, you should be kept aware of developments in the case and of any dates (and changes in any dates) when you're required to appear in court. You should also expect to have the sentence explained to you and to be notified when the offender is released or paroled. Cooperating with the police and prosecuting attorney may help bring the defendant to justice and may help bring closure to issues you're dealing with as a result of the crime.

One of the most important issues for any victim, particularly in situations involving violent crimes, is feeling safe while the defendant is being prosecuted. The court can issue a **restraining order**, in certain circumstances, which means that the court will order the defendant to have no contact with you and to be subject to penalities if the order is violated. Unfortunately, these orders are of questionable value because they rely on the defendant to obey the court's order.

If I've been injured or the victim of a crime, can I bring a personal lawsuit against the perpetrator?

Yes you can, but that case would have to be in civil court, not in criminal court. Only the government can serve as the plaintiff in a criminal case. In a civil case, you can try to recover damages or compensation for the harm you suffered, be it physical, emotional, or financial.

What if I don't want to get involved in a lawsuit? Are there organizations that help victims deal with the effects of a crime?

The National Center for Victims of Crime—at 211 Wilson Boulevard, Suite 300, Arlington, VA 22201, 703-276-2880 (**www.nvc.org**)—is an advocate and support center for victims of crime and their families. It includes a host of valuable resources including a toll-free help line: 800-FYI-CALL.

FIRST PERSON DISASTER STORY

Mistaken Identity

When I got a threatening letter from someone who I had never heard from saying all these terrible things I had done, I was surprised. Then I realized it had been sent to the wrong address; it was to my neighbor who has a similar last name. I forwarded the letter and thought it was over. A week later I started getting threatening phone calls. I finally had to call the police, who tracked the guy down. All I wanted was for the police to tell this nut that he had the wrong person. I learned then that harassment is serious business, and I had to bring charges to make it stop. —Michael T.

now what do I do?
Answers to common questions

If I hire a lawyer, am I stuck with him?

Not really. You can certainly interview more than one lawyer until you find one you like; but bear in mind that once you've hired one, it can be complicated and potentially harmful to your case to change lawyers midway. That said, if you can't work with your attorney and the relationship has broken down, you can fire him and hire a new one.

What will determine whether a young person is tried as an adult or as a minor?

The state will consider the seriousness of the crime and the past criminal record of the defendant. For example, for some of the most serious crimes, like murder or rape, some states would try the offender as an adult as long as he's above a certain age.

I've heard that there are some instances when a parent is held responsible for a minor child's criminal behavior. When does that happen?

Very rarely. Generally, a parent is held responsible when the parent has engaged in criminal negligence—for example, when a child injures someone by using a gun that was carelessly stored where the child had easy access to it.

Will my lawyer decide whether I should take a plea bargain?

No. It's always your right to decide whether to plead guilty or not. Your lawyer can merely tell you based on his experience what he recommends given the facts of your case. If you don't trust your lawyer's opinion on this, you may not have hired the right lawyer and may need to get another one. Your liberty is at stake, so it's very important that you have confidence in your lawyer.

now where do I go?!

CONTACTS

www.nolo.com — within the criminal section you can search the "Frequently Asked Questions," "Legal Dictionary," and "Encyclopedia."

www.law.cornell.edu — hosted by the law library of Cornell University's law school, this site is a great place to find primary source material like statutes and case law, summaries of each area of the law, and links to other useful sites.

www. freeadvice.com — look under the comprehensive criminal section for the commonly asked questions and answers. The site also offers live online chats with criminal lawyers during specified hours.

BOOKS

**The Criminal Law Handbook:
Know Your Rights, Survive the System**
by Paul Bergman
and Sara J. Berman-Barrett

Understanding Criminal Law
by Joshua Dressler

Money and Credit

money trouble

What a bankruptcy lawyer can do

How to find a bankruptcy lawyer

Personal recommendations are always the best way to find a lawyer. Talk to people you know who have used a bankruptcy lawyer or ask professionals like certified public accountants (CPAs), financial planners, or life insurance brokers, all of whom have contact with bankruptcy attorneys. If that's not fruitful, contact your local bar association or search a lawyers' directory like Martindale-Hubbell (available at some libraries or on the Internet at **www.martindale.com**) or **www.findlaw.com**, both of which list lawyers by specialty and location.

Money. You earn it, you spend it, and hopefully you save a bit of it along the way. So why would you need a lawyer? For many people, the tricky part involves borrowing it (commonly referred to as incurring debt) or spending too much and getting in trouble with a debt-collection agency. If you get too far in debt, you may need to declare **bankruptcy** (a legal process that gives debtors protection from their creditors while debt is being paid or forgiven, for more information, see pages 146–149). In any of these scenarios, you may ultimately find you need a lawyer.

Even if your situation isn't serious enough to send you to bankruptcy court, a bankruptcy lawyer is probably the best type of lawyer to see because they are generally the lawyers most familiar with legal issues relating to debt.

However, be wary of offers to make your credit troubles disappear, whether those offers are made by e-mail, regular mail, telephone, or any other method. Bad credit cannot simply be erased, and credit-repair services often charge a lot of money to do things you can do yourself, such as contacting a credit-reporting agency, obtaining a copy of your credit report, or sending letters to people you owe disputing incorrect information.

Do you need a lawyer—or just a good accountant?

The time to see a lawyer is when a financial event has occurred that can have a dramatic effect on your life, such as your bank threatening to take away your house because you are behind on mortgage payments, your bank account being frozen, or someone obtaining a court judgment against you (e.g., a court order requiring you to pay damages in a lawsuit). For events like a divorce or an extended period of disability, your accountant or a good financial planner should be able to help you.

Questions to ask a bankruptcy lawyer

Before you hire a lawyer, here are a few questions you should ask in an initial interview:

How much time do you spend on bankruptcy cases?

How many years of experience do you have, and are you board certified by the American Bankruptcy Institute?

Do you specialize in representing debtors (those who owe money) or creditors (those who collect money)? You'll want someone who specializes in debtors.

Will I need to file bankruptcy, or are there other options?

What effect would a bankruptcy have on my credit?

Will all my debts go away if I go through bankruptcy?

How do you charge? Most bankruptcy lawyers require payment up front before the case is filed, as it is the only way they can be assured of getting paid. In some instances lawyers will accept installment payments, so don't be afraid to ask.

types of debt

Know what you're
getting into

During the course of their lives, most people take on **debt**—the term used to cover the various ways in which money is lent to someone with an agreement to repay it. No matter what it is used for, debt comes at a price—in the form of **interest**, a percentage of the total loan (or **principal**) paid each month to the lender. Typically, each debt payment is part principal and part interest.

The most common types of debt are secured and unsecured debt. The distinction is especially important to understand if you're having problems making payments.

Secured Debt

When debt is secured, a lender holds as collateral the property for which a loan is being made. If a borrower **defaults** (fails to make timely payments), the lender has the right to take back that property. The most common debts in this category are real estate and car loans. If you default after a certain number of payments, you will likely not only lose the item involved but also may lose any payments you have made until the time of your default.

Unsecured Debt

Unsecured debt is merely a promise by a borrower to repay a lender for a loan. With unsecured debt, the rights of the lender (also known as a creditor) are much more limited than those of a lender with a secured debt. Common examples of unsecured debts are credit card debt, department store's revolving lines of credit, personal bank and credit union loans. If you fail to make timely payments on an unsecured debt, the only remedy for the lender is to sue you to try to obtain a judgment against you.

ASK THE EXPERTS

Do I need a lawyer to get a loan?

You may need a lawyer if you're buying a house (see pages 30–53) or getting a loan to start a business (see pages 168–187). But you won't need one for most other loans. Once you have a loan, if you get to a point where you can't make the payments or some other dramatic event has occurred (e.g., your car has been repossessed, or your house is about to be foreclosed), that would be the time to get a lawyer involved.

I'm receiving offers to consolidate my debt at reduced interest rates. Is this a good idea?

Be careful about these offers, especially if your debt is mostly from credit cards, (unsecured debt). The interest they charge can be higher than what you're already paying. Often, people suggest consolidating your debts by getting a second mortgage. But be careful if consolidation means converting unsecured debt to secured debt, because if you can't make these new consolidated payments, you could lose your home. Talk it over with your lawyer before doing this—bankruptcy may be a better option.

I've taken out a student loan to cover my college tuition. What will happen if I have trouble repaying this loan?

You should be able to modify the terms of your loan by contacting your administrator. You may be able to extend the repayment period and reduce the monthly amount due. Whatever you do, don't just stop paying—you could subject yourself to higher interest payments. You may also be able to consolidate your loans and lower your interest rate in exchange for a longer payback period.

dealing with creditors

What happens if you can't pay

After getting a loan, what happens if you have trouble making the payments on time? If it's just one payment, call the lender and explain you will be paying late. If you haven't missed a payment before, lenders may be willing to negotiate with you. But if you miss several payments, you can expect your lender (or a debt collector hired by the lender) to call or send you a letter with a subtle (or not so subtle) message that if you don't do something about your delinquency, they will take further action.

Before you get too anxious about this, you'll be given plenty of notice as well as the opportunity to do something about it. Drastic measures like **repossession** (when a lender takes back a piece of property, like a car, against which you had borrowed money), **foreclosure** (when a lender takes possession of your house and evicts you), or **wage garnishment** (when the holder of a court judgment has a portion of your salary deducted to pay your debts) don't happen unless you're seriously in default or have neglected a debt for quite a long time. As long as you don't ignore your creditors, they may be willing to listen to and consider a request for relief. They would usually prefer to negotiate with you for a different payment plan than take back property that secures a debt or bring a lawsuit against you.

When you tell a creditor that you can't make your scheduled payments, explain the reason for your financial problems and how long you think they will last. If you've just lost your job, gotten divorced, or had some other devastating financial event, creditors can be reasonable. Next, come up with a proposal for the type of relief that will help you get back on your feet. Don't make promises you can't keep. If you default on a revised payment plan, collection efforts typically will resume, possibly with more intensity.

If things get really bad—because you decided not to negotiate, have been unsuccessful at negotiating, or are simply unable to pay—it's a good idea to see a lawyer.

ASK THE EXPERTS

If a creditor sues me and obtains a judgment, is it true that part of my paycheck can go to my creditor without my consent?

It sure is. A **wage garnishment** order is a method of enforced collection in which a court determines that a creditor can have your employer withhold part of your wages. The underlying debt can be anything from delinquent spousal or child support payments to a long ignored tax obligation. Each state regulates the percentage of your wages that can be garnished—and the laws are designed to leave you with enough to feed, clothe, and house your family.

I've heard that debt collectors can't call me at the office—is that true? How else are they restricted?

Generally, state law requires that debt collectors not use deceptive or abusive practices, including failing to identify themselves as debt collectors. Nor can they make calls to debtors at the workplace. Debt collectors are prohibited from using obscene or threatening language. These restrictions apply to third-party debt collectors (collection agencies) and not just to the lender itself. If you believe a debt collector has violated the law, you can report the violation to your state attorney general's office or the Federal Trade Commission, which enforce the laws governing debt collectors.

your credit history

Know your rights

You may be surprised to find out that what goes on between you and your creditors isn't private. How you behave with one creditor affects the type of loan you may be able to get from others, as well as your ability to get insurance, a job, or even rent an apartment. This is because companies called credit-reporting agencies track people's credit history and create records known as credit reports from such data. The reports are sold to banks or other institutions that need to assess a person's creditworthiness.

Credit reporting agencies are regulated by a federal law called the Fair Credit Reporting Act (FCRA), which also gives certain rights to consumers. Here are a few things you should know about credit reports and your rights under the FCRA:

- Lenders do not need to notify you if they report information about your payment history to a credit-reporting agency.

- If you've been denied credit, insurance, or employment-based information from your credit report, the entity denying you credit must give you the name, address, and telephone number of the credit-reporting agency that issued the credit report.

- You can obtain a copy of your credit report by contacting one of the major credit reporting agencies (see pages 144–145). By law they can charge up to $8 to send you the report. You can get one free copy under certain circumstances, such as:
  - you're unemployed
  - you're on welfare
  - your credit report is inaccurate because of fraud.

- If there are errors in your credit report, both the credit-reporting agency and the provider of the incorrect information are required to change it, as long as you notify them in writing. Keep copies of everything you send and use certified mail.

What if there's a mistake in my credit report—can I get it fixed?

Yes, you can. Write a letter to the credit bureau and tell them about the error. Send a copy of your letter to the lender who gave out the erroneous information. A summary of your complaint will be put in your credit-report file. If the lender who gave out the wrong information doesn't respond to or dispute your claim within 30 days, the credit bureau must delete the error from your report.

How can I rebuild my credit?

The best way to rebuild your credit is to pay all your bills in full and on time—never paying just the minimum amount due, and never incurring interest charges or late fees. Another option is to get a debit card. These are issued by banks and look exactly like a credit card but allow you to make charges based on the funds available in your account. This won't necessarily help your credit, but it will avoid some of the cost associated with credit cards (and the embarrassment many people face by not having one).

FIRST PERSON DISASTER STORY

Getting back on my feet

My husband and I were married for 5 years, during which he racked up all kinds of debt through his poor financial planning. Before my marriage, my credit history was perfect. After we got divorced, I was worried that I wouldn't be able to get a car loan or obtain other credit because of the mess he got us into. Then I realized I never signed the contracts for any of our credit cards, which he insisted should be in his name and which he never let me use. Boy, was I lucky—I was able to borrow the money I needed to get back on my feet. I'm told that the money we did manage to accumulate together could be used to pay down his debts. Thankfully, I've kept some of my own money separate, including an inheritance that I recently received, so that at least is mine and can't be used by him. I'm also alerting all our creditors so that going forward my credit won't be impacted further by his debts. —Dorothy A.

the credit report

**Unraveling
your rating**

A credit report is a public record of your history of paying your debts. Your credit information is gathered by companies called credit bureaus that sell it to anyone with a legitimate interest in giving you credit—for example, a bank or a credit card company. There are three main companies that report on consumers' credit (see box). What's in the report? A list of how much money you've borrowed and from which institution; whether you made payments on time or ever missed a payment; whether you've ever filed for bankruptcy; whether you ever had a **credit lien** (a creditor's claim against your property, usually your house); whether you've paid your taxes; and whether there are any outstanding judgments against you.

Based on this information, they give you a **credit rating** or a formal evaluation of your credit history and your ability to repay future debt. Some bureaus issue a score between 300 (the worst) and 900 (the best), which is assigned to you based on the amount of money you borrowed and the way you repaid it. Most lenders won't lend to you if your score is under 640; a score above 700 is considered good. Some credit bureaus simply note where you missed or were late with a payment, which immediately triggers concern.

A credit bureau sells a copy of your credit report to any institution, such as a bank, credit card issuer, or mortgage company, whenever you apply for a loan. (Sometimes they give it to a prospective employer, too). If your credit rating is good, you'll get the most favorable rates available. If not, then fixing your credit report should become your number one priority. And if it needs fixing, you're not alone. About 70% of consumers in the United States have at least one negative item in their credit reports. If you can explain the problem—say, a missed credit card payment due to a hospital stay—you can write down your explanation in 100 words or less and submit copies of it to the three major credit bureaus, and they will attach it to your file. Bad items, such as filing for bankruptcy, stay on your report for 10 years.

How can I get my credit report?

Write to these three major credit bureaus and ask for a copy. Usually you must pay a small fee.

Experian
(formerly TRW Information Services)
P.O. Box 949
Allen, TX 75013
888-397-3742
www.experian.com

Equifax Information Services
P.O. Box 740256
Atlanta, GA 30374
800-997-2493
www.equifax.com

Trans Union
P.O. Box 2000
Chester, PA 19022
800-888-4213
www.transunion.com

CREDIT REPORT

EQUIFAX

Please address all future correspondence to:

Equifax Credit Information Services
P. O. Box 105518
Atlanta, GA 30348
1(800) 882-0648

Personal Identification Information

John Jones
100 Main Street
Beecher, NY 00000

January 15, 1999

Social Security #: 000-00-000
Date of Birth: March 7th, 1955

Credit Account Information

Company Name	Account Number	Whose Acct	Date Opened	Months Reviewed	Date of Last Activity	High Credit	Terms	Items as of Date Reported			Date Reported
								Balance	Past Due	Status	
American Express	00000000000	I	08/86	1	08/98	$0		$0		01	08/98
American Express PAID ACCOUNT/ZERO BALANCE ACCOUNT CLOSED BY CONSUMER	00000000000	I	01/96	4	05/96	$7000		$0		R	06/96
American Residential REAL ESTATE MORTGAGE	00000000000	S	07/88	61	11/94	$41300	380	$0		I1	11/94
Atlantic Mortgage Previous Payment History: 2 Times 90 + days late Previous Status: 07/97 - I5; 06/97 - I5 FORECLOSURE PROCESS STARTED PAID ACCOUNT/ZERO BALANCE	00000000000	I	04/87	2	12/96	$41300	385	$0		I5	01/99
Bank Boston AUTO	00000000000	I	05/93	7	12/93	$7850	207	$0		I1	01/94
UNIS Cash Reserve LINE OF CREDIT AMOUNT IN H/C COLUMN IS CREDIT LIMIT	00000000000		12/94	46	11/98	$2500		$0		R1	11/98
UNIS Home Mortgage Previous Payment History: 1 Time 30 days late Previous Status: 02/97 - I2 ACCOUNT TRANSFERRED OR SOLD REAL ESTATE MORTGAGE	00000000000	I	04/87	26	12/96	$41300	385	$0		I2	03/97
UNIS Manhattan Bank LINE OF CREDIT AMOUNT IN H/C COLUMN IS CREDIT LIMIT	00000000000	J	08/92	48	11/98	$3500	109	$3101		R1	12/98
UNIS Manhattan Bank HOME EQUITY LINE OF CREDIT	00000000000	J	06/96	28	11/98	$73810		$39772		R1	11/98

Creditors will look for any instances of late payments, among other things.

145

bankruptcy basics

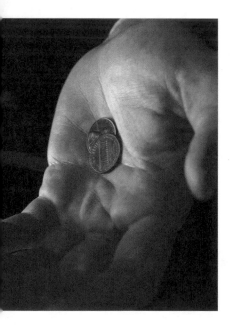

Bankruptcy has an ominous ring, but it can be good news for people who have gotten themselves into more debt than they can handle. Bankruptcy is often a way for consumers to get a "fresh start" on their financial lives.

Most bankruptcy cases occur because a consumer has reached an intolerable level of unsecured debt (see page 138 for an explanation of secured versus unsecured debts), usually involving credit cards. Credit card borrowing (which occurs if you charge more than you can afford to pay on your credit card) is one of the easiest ways to get into serious debt. That's because credit cards charge high interest rates. Once you start overspending on your credit card, it's very hard to ever get above water.

As long as you meet the necessary legal requirements, bankruptcy may be the way for you to say good-bye to credit card or other debt that you're unable to pay. Of course there are downsides to bankruptcy, like going through a period where it's difficult to get credit. But for many people, the benefits far outweigh the burdens. The further you can put bankruptcy behind you, the more possible it is to experience complete financial recovery, provided you pay all your bills on time.

How bankruptcy works
There are a few different types of bankruptcy, and it's important to understand the distinctions.

Chapter 7
Chapter 7 bankruptcy, known as **liquidation**, is by far the most common type used by consumers. The bankruptcy court appoints a trustee who locates all of the assets you own, sells those assets, and distributes the money available to your creditors. At the end of a liquidation, you would receive a **discharge**, which means your unsecured debts are eliminated.

Depending on where you live, the following items (called **exemptions**) may be protected by a bankruptcy: equity in your home; furniture; furnishings and appliances; clothing and personal effects; automobiles; tools of your trade or occupation; and retirement benefits. The extent to which each of these is protected varies by state.

Chapter 11

This type of bankruptcy, known as **reorganization**, is used primarily by businesses but can also be used by individuals. Chapter 11 can be time-consuming and expensive. The goal is to come up with a plan to pay your creditors by reducing your payments significantly or extending them over a longer period of time, or both. This is sometimes a good option for individuals who have significant assets beyond the exemptions or who feel compelled to pay something on their debts.

Chapter 13

Chapter 13 is a way for individuals to restructure their debts through what is known as a wage-earner plan. It's something like Chapter 11 except it is only available to those with secured debts of less than $807,750 and unsecured debts of less than $269,250 (note that these numbers will change because they are tied to the cost of living). It is also faster and less expensive than Chapter 11. The other advantage to to Chapter 13 is that it allows you to eliminate more types of debt than Chapter 7 or 11.

In Chapter 13, you dedicate all of your discretionary income to paying off debts. Most Chapter 13 bankruptcies are completed within 3 to 5 years. At the end of that time, you will have paid off a percentage of your total debt and receive a discharge—which means the rest of your debt will be forgiven.

Making bankruptcy more difficult

In recent years, there's been a considerable effort in Congress to revise the bankruptcy laws to make it more difficult for consumers to take advantage of protection from creditors. You can learn more about this by visiting the Web site of the American Bankruptcy Institute at **www.abiworld.org.**

filing for bankruptcy

When do you need a lawyer?

There is no requirement to use a lawyer to file for bankruptcy, but you'll probably want one, since there is often strategy involved in filing for bankruptcy, and an experienced attorney can help you come out of it in the best financial shape possible. She can also help determine whether you should file under Chapter 7, 11, or 13 (see pages 146–147).

How a bankruptcy lawyer gets paid

If you retain a lawyer to represent you in bankruptcy, your lawyer will have to be paid up front (otherwise whatever you owe would be discharged in the bankruptcy proceeding and your lawyer won't get paid). Often, the lawyer will accept installment

payments and file for bankruptcy only after the fee is paid in full. Some lawyers may even agree to accept an installment plan that continues past the bankruptcy filing, but this is not very common.

What to do if you're broke

If you can't afford a lawyer, there are bankruptcy preparers who are not licensed to practice law but are trained to assist in the paperwork for a bankruptcy. You have to be very careful when using one of these as they do not provide any legal advice—they merely prepare the necessary forms for filing. If you have absolutely no assets worth protecting and are trying to economize, you may wish to look into using one of these services. On the other hand, if you have any significant assets, it would be a good idea to work with a lawyer who can apply strategies that help protect them.

When bankruptcy isn't an option

Bankruptcy protection is generally not available to those who have received a discharge in bankruptcy in the prior six years.

Will all debts be forgiven in bankruptcy?

Certain debts cannot be eliminated in any bankruptcy. They include: taxes; money received under false pretenses; money received by fraud, embezzlement, or theft; spousal and child support obligations; debts resulting from willful and malicious injury to another (e.g., assault and battery); fines imposed for violating the law; educational loans (with some exceptions), and debts related to death or injury resulting from drunk driving. In a Chapter 7 bankruptcy, you'll still have these debts at the completion of the bankruptcy; in a Chapter 11 or 13, you pay them as part of your bankruptcy plan.

Can bankruptcy get rid of my gambling debts?

It depends. The bankruptcy judge will weigh your debts very carefully. For instance, if you genuinely have a gambling problem and have acquired your debts over a period of time, the debt might be discharged. But it's less likely they would be if you went to Vegas on a whim, got a line of credit, and engaged in a one-night spending spree.

What will my financial future be like after bankruptcy?

From one perspective it will look good, because you will have eliminated or greatly reduced the amount of debt you have. On the other hand, for the first year or two after bankruptcy, it may be impossible to get any credit at all; and when you do, it will be at a very high interest rate. The farther away from your bankruptcy you get, the easier it will become, provided you pay all your bills on time. After 10 years, the bankruptcy will disappear from your credit report and you won't need to explain it at all. Keep in mind that if you're ever asked the question,"Have you ever filed for bankruptcy?" you may be committing a federal crime if you don't answer yes.

now what do I do?

Answers to common questions

If I'm in debt, should I delay paying my taxes in order to pay off other bills?

Absolutely not. Taxes should be a priority. Tax obligations can become **tax liens** (a means by which the IRS can seize any of your property to satisfy the taxes due). This can quickly destroy your credit.

I often receive offers for secured credit cards in the mail. What are these and should I consider getting one?

Secured credit cards are a way for people with poor credit to obtain a credit card. They usually require you to put up the dollar amount equivalent to the credit being made available (if you put $1000 in a bank account, you can charge up to $1000 on a credit card the bank issues you). To the outside world, secured credit cards look like a typical credit card. The disadvantages are that there are often fees involved in obtaining one, the money securing the credit will generally earn very little interest, and you will likely be subject to high interest rates if you are even one day late on a payment.

Someone has been using my Social Security number and obtaining credit cards under my name. I'm now getting bills for all kinds of charges I didn't incur. What can I do?

This is called identity theft. There are several steps you can take on your own to stop it. First, contact the fraud department at the major credit bureaus (see page 144) and alert them that someone has fraudulently been using your identity. Ask them to put a "fraud alert" on your file so that no new credit can be extended without your approval. Next, file a police report with your local police department. If you've learned of any particular institutions (e.g., credit card companies, banks, department stores) where fraudulent accounts have been opened using your name, alert them of the problem. Contact the Identity Theft Clearinghouse for more information, at 877-ID-THEFT. As long as you report the incident immediately upon discovering that your card has been stolen, under federal law you will only be liable for up to $50 of unauthorized charges on any one credit card.

Will I need a lawyer if I'm audited by the IRS?

Probably not. The accountant who prepared your return is the best person to represent you during an audit. Audit notices generally target a particular tax year and a specific issue such as a business expense or a charitable deduction. If the case is not a routine audit and there are serious issues involved (such as a failure to file tax returns or an under reporting of income), you'll probably want to be represented by a lawyer.

now where do I go?!

CONTACTS

www.nolo.com — comprehensive information and answers to commonly asked questions are provided in the "Debt and Bankruptcy" section.

www.findlaw.com — legal portrait with content customized to legal professionals, students, public, and businesses. In the "Public" section, look under "Money" for resources.

www.freeAdvice.com — offers an extensive question and answer section under the "Bankruptcy" heading, as well as live online chats with lawyers during specified hours.

www.ftc.gov — the Federal Trade Commission enforces a variety of consumer protection laws including those that regulate fair debt collection practices.

www.myvesta.org — a nonprofit financial services organization that offers nationwide credit and financial assistance to consumers.

BOOKS

Debt-Proof Living
by Mary Hunt

I Haven't Saved a Dime, Now What?!
by Barbara Loos

Money Troubles: Legal Strategies to Cope With Your Debts
by Robin Leonard

Bankruptcy: Is It the Right Solution to Your Debt Problems?
by Robin Leonard

Slash Your Debt: Save Money and Secure Your Future
by Gerri Detweiler, Marc Eisenson, and Nancy Castleman

Wills and Trusts

Know Everyone by these Presents,

as princ

That I,

and stead,

hereditaments that

and all of suc

assessed or

er with or wit
ts, or of any pa
or other structu
ands;

es now or hereaf
rty belonging to
s, or to make, sig
ment agreement or
or necessary to ac

Power of Attorney

nsealed,

nature or description whatsoever, on any of r
ion with the management, use or occupation
nd/or in respect of the rents, issues and profit
proofs of all loss or losses sustained or claim
same, and to make, execute and deliver rece.
erwise.

cover and receive all goods, claims, debts,
nay hereafter be due or belong to me (inclu
for the recovery of any land, buildings, te
he possession whereof I may be entitled) a
discharges therefor, under seal or otherwis

pt, collect and deliver any or all bills of

time or times, that may hereafter be own
acceptance, made, executed, endorsed, acc
aid attorney;

res of stock, bonds or
or ass

estate planning

Preparing for the future

How to find an estate planning lawyer

If you know anyone who has drawn up a will and been pleased with the lawyer, ask for the lawyer's name. Also talk to professionals you respect, like insurance brokers, accountants, or other lawyers. If you can't get a personal recommendation, contact your local bar association or search in a lawyers' directory like Martindale-Hubbell (available at some libraries and on the Internet at **www.martin dale.com**). The Web site **www.findlaw.com** also lists lawyers by specialty and geographic location.

Many people reach adulthood and don't bother to write a will—after all, none of us wants to think about our own mortality. So what kinds of things signal it's time to think about managing your **estate**—the personal belongings, real estate, and financial assets you own?

Say you're about to have your first child and want to name a **guardian**—someone who would take care of your child if you and your spouse died. Perhaps you just got married, you've inherited a sum of money, bought a house, or your financial situation has dramatically changed. Any of these situations, or countless others, indicate that it's a good time to write or change your will or think about managing your estate.

Estate planning lawyers, also called "wills and trusts" or "trusts and estates" specialists, can advise you about making sure your wishes are carried out when you're no longer around. These lawyers can also help you deal with the legal issues surrounding getting older and illnesses—issues you may be grappling with either for yourself or for family members. Estate laws vary from state to state, so be sure to consult a lawyer licensed to practice in your state as well as in a state where property you own is located.

Questions to ask an estate planning lawyer

How much of your practice focuses on estate planning?
Estate planning can have serious financial and tax implications. Unless you have an extremely simple estate, you'll probably want to talk to someone who is a specialist in this area.

How long have you been practicing this area of law?
While you may feel comfortable (and pay less) with a young lawyer just getting his feet wet, an estate lawyer with years of experience may be the best way to go. Someone who has worked with many families over time will generally be able to offer you solid advice about thorny issues.

What do you expect to accomplish for me?
A good estate planning lawyer will do her best to understand your thoughts on issues such as passing down wealth, minimizing taxes on your estate, as well as the nuances of your own family situation. If you feel a lawyer is not listening to you or is not interested in your particular needs, that lawyer probably isn't a good fit for you.

How do you charge?
Fees will vary widely based on your geographic location and the size and complexity of your estate. Typically, fees will be on an hourly basis, but some lawyers may be willing to work with you for a fixed fee.

creating a will

A little legal know-how before you leap

In order to understand the basics of estate planning, there are some concepts you should become familiar with. Here's a primer to get you started:

A **will** is a document that explains how you want your property and certain family relationships to be managed after your death. In order to be legally valid, a will must meet certain requirements, which vary by state, but in most cases it must be:

- a written document
- created by an adult of sound mind (called a **testator**)
- signed by the testator and witnessed by others.

These requirements are designed to ensure that people know what they are doing when they write a will and are not improperly influenced by others.

When creating a will, you'll be asked to appoint a person, called an **executor**, who will act as the administrator of your will. The executor will be your voice in the process of handling your estate; so the person you choose—often a trusted family member, lawyer, or friend—should be someone you believe would make decisions consistent with what you would have done if you were alive.

A will usually covers two things: the distribution of assets held in your own name (including cash and other financial assets, real estate, personal property like jewelry and other valuables, and anything else you've acquired during your life); and the care of people, usually minors or those unable to care for themselves. Wills can be as basic or detailed as the desires of the writer, and while there are common ways to distribute property, a will can deviate from all norms and still be considered valid.

Can I write my own will?

Yes, you can, but it's not advisable, because you run the risk of creating an invalid will. Simply writing a "will" and signing it does not make it a will. There are formalities that must be followed. These vary by state, but they will include things like the number of witnesses, whether it needs to be **notarized** (witnessed and signed by a person authorized by your state for specific purposes), or whether a separate **affidavit** (a sworn statement) regarding execution of the will is also needed. Also, handwritten wills are not valid in many states.

Do I need a will in order to name a guardian for my children?

Probably not, although you should talk with a lawyer to make sure you name a guardian in a way that complies with the requirements of your state. Most states have procedures for naming a guardian for minor children—often with formalities like having the document signed before witnesses or a **notary** (a person licensed by your state to witness such signings). That said, if you're going to the trouble of appointing a guardian, you might as well take care of your will at the same time.

FIRST PERSON   DISASTER STORY

When the will didn't count

I had always dreamed of living in the home I grew up in. After Mom died, Dad remarried but promised me that he had arranged for the home to be mine. After his death, I was shocked to learn that his wife was selling it. It seems that Dad had specified in his will that the house should go to me upon his death, but because he'd made the house jointly owned with his wife, the instructions in his will didn't count and the house went to her. —Andrew T.

what's probate?

How your assets get to the right heir

How do your assets get distributed to your heirs and your debts get paid off? In most cases, it's through **probate** court. The job of the probate court is to make sure your will is valid (signed and witnessed correctly), that all taxes and outstanding debts have been paid, and all your wishes carried out. (You can talk to your lawyer about the ways to avoid the probate process.)

During probate, the court will appoint a personal representative, usually the person you've named as the **executor** in your will. It's the executor's job to see the case through court, usually with the help of an attorney, and to carry out the wishes stated in your will.

Some key responsibilities of your executor are to:

- Open and inventory your safe deposit box according to the laws of the state.

- Get copies of the death certificate.

- Provide the court with an inventory of all assets held in your name that do not pass by contract (e.g., insurance, joint and survivor accounts).

- Process payments of taxes, and any valid claims of creditors, including funeral expenses and bills from last illness.

- Notify the Social Security Administration of the death, and find out whether any survivor benefits are available.

- Employ any necessary professionals needed to assist, such as lawyers and accountants.

- Distribute assets according to the terms of the will.

- Make funeral arrangements, if the family hasn't done it.

- Put a death notice in the local paper if the family so desires.

Tax concerns

Keep in mind that your estate may be subject to federal and/or state taxes (including estate or inheritance taxes, as well as taxes on income earned by the estate assets during administration of the estate). A good estate planning lawyer will be able to help you understand the tax implications of your estate. In fact, in estates with substantial assets, the major work done by a lawyer is tax planning. This area of the law has recently undergone and will continue to undergo substantial changes.

ASK THE EXPERTS

If I'm named as an executor in a will, am I obligated to use the law firm that drafted the will for the probating of the estate?

Absolutely not, even if the will seems to suggest otherwise.

How long does the probate process usually take?

Estates are usually administered within a year, but complications in such matters as locating heirs, disposing of a business or real estate, or giving notice to the people who would inherit if there were no will (**heirs at law**), can cause it to drag on much longer. During the probate process, the assets are not necessarily tied up. Partial distributions can be made to heirs as long as the executor is satisfied that there are sufficient assets remaining to take care of all expenses, debts, and taxes. Estate tax returns are typically due nine months from the date of death.

I would like my heirs to be able to avoid probate completely. How can I make that happen?

One of the things probate does is transfer ownership of goods from you to your heirs. To avoid that procedure, set up your finances so that transfer happens immediately upon your death. For example, you can change the title to property from just your name to either joint tenancy or tenancy by the entirety. There are, however, two things to be aware of with joint holdings: first, such accounts are subject to the creditors of the person you set up the joint account with; and, second, by creating joint assets, you're sharing control of those funds with your joint owner. You also can set up pay-on-death accounts. To do that, make sure all your bank accounts, government securities, and investment securities have a designated beneficiary of your choosing. The money remains in your complete control until your death. Perhaps a better way to avoid probate is to set up a living trust (see page 160).

setting up a trust

Another way to distribute your assets

Another important estate planning tool is a **trust**, a legal entity created to hold assets on behalf of another. You can create a trust as part of your will (a **testamentary trust**), or as a separate document in order to manage some or all of your assets during your lifetime (known as an **inter vivos** or living trust).

In either case, there will be a trust agreement prepared by a lawyer that will contain certain essential elements. The person whose assets fund the trust is called a **trustor, settlor,** or **grantor**. In order to be valid, a trust also must have a **trustee** or **co-trustees**, individuals chosen by the trustor to administer the trust, as well as a **successor trustee**, someone who would serve as trustee in the event that the trustee is unable to do so.

The **beneficiaries** are the people on whose behalf the trust assets are held. The trust agreement will outline, among other things: the purpose of the trust (e.g., for education and support of the beneficiaries), the name of the trustees and successor trustees, and the trustor's desires for how the trust income and principal are to be managed and distributed.

Why create a trust?

There are many reasons. People use trusts to put aside assets to care for those who can't take care of themselves (like a minor child or someone who is ill), to ensure that the operation of a business will not be interrupted, or to make a charitable gift. A trust can also allow funds to be released over time, rather than all at once—something that's useful for preserving assets. A trust for the benefit of a minor child can provide considerable savings.

Unless the trust is itself part of a will, the assets in it need not go through the probate process—which means that they can be distributed more quickly and inexpensively than through a will. There are also certain tax benefits to using a trust. For these reasons, trusts have become increasingly popular, sometimes replacing a will almost entirely. Trusts are complicated, however, so make sure to talk them through with your lawyer.

I want to provide for my son in my will but fear he wouldn't be able to manage the money properly if he received an inheritance all at once. What can I do?

You can create a trust that will give a trustee power to manage the assets contained in the trust and advance funds to your son according to whatever instructions you provide. You can also give your trustee the discretion to distribute a portion or all of the money when the trustee feels your son is capable of managing his own funds.

What if I set up a trust and the trustee doesn't follow the terms of the trust?

The beneficiary of the trust can go to court to seek enforcement of the terms of the trust or even remove a trustee. If the beneficiary is a minor or otherwise unable to bring a case, the court can appoint a guardian to bring the suit.

I want to leave a large chunk of money to charity and worry that my family will challenge such a donation after I'm gone. Will my wishes be honored if I set up a trust?

If it's in your will, it shouldn't be an issue (although talk to your lawyer about the legal issues involved in making gifts to charitable institutions). Of course, when you appoint a trustee, that person should be someone you trust and who fully understands your wishes. It's also a good idea to notify the institution of your intentions before you die. If the institution is expecting a gift, it will be much more difficult for someone to interfere with your wishes.

powers of attorney and guardians

Appointing someone to act on your behalf

In addition to trusts, there are other ways to give someone the power to act on your behalf—say, if you developed an illness that might ultimately affect your ability to function, or you want to name someone to care for your children if something happens to you and the other parent.

The most common way to give rights to another person is through a legal document called a **power of attorney**, which appoints someone to act in your place for whatever purpose you indicate. When you issue a power of attorney, you are considered the **principal** and the person you appoint is your **agent** or your **attorney-in-fact**. An agent can only act with the permission of the principal.

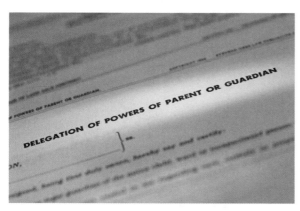

A **durable power of attorney** is one that remains valid even if the principal loses the capacity to direct the agent. If you developed a mentally debilitating disease like Alzheimer's, for example, but prior to your becoming ill you had issued a durable power of attorney to someone, then the person holding the power of attorney would be able to act on your behalf. The key is that the power must be granted while you are still of sound mind.

Another area in which legal responsibility is granted to someone else involves minor children or adults who are unable to care for themselves. Here's where court-appointed guardians come in. A **guardian** is an official agent of the court who is appointed to oversee the personal and/or financial affairs of a minor or person otherwise unable to care for himself. A minor child with one surviving parent has a "natural" guardian and won't need a court-appointed guardian. Guardianships are established through a petition to the court. You can use your will to nominate the person you choose to serve in that role, or you can use another separate document such as a power of attorney.

What if I give someone a power of attorney and then want to change my mind. Can I nullify it and transfer it to someone else?

Definitely. And because you may change your mind about a power of attorney, it's never a good idea to give away the original document. When you issue a new power of attorney, you should get back any copies of prior powers you have issued and make sure that the new document states that all prior powers are revoked.

Do I need a lawyer to issue a power of attorney?

Not really. Power of attorney forms are found in stationery stores that sell legal forms. Make sure that if you fill out a preprinted power of attorney form, it is properly executed for your state. Because requirements can vary considerably, it's a good idea to have a lawyer do a quick review even if you're using a form document.

Can I name more than one guardian for my children?

Many people choose a married couple as co-guardians, but it's much less common to choose two people as co-guardians when they aren't living together and sharing a household. Even when choosing a couple, you should indicate which person should be responsible if the couple is not still married at the time they become co-guardians. You should also name a successor guardian, someone who can serve if your guardian is unable to serve.

healthcare and elder-care issues

Documents to help direct your treatment

Since health problems are almost inevitable, it pays to think about what would happen if you or a loved one needed medical care and were unable to properly direct that treatment. The law offers some tools to help.

One option is appointing someone as an agent authorized to make choices about your medical treatment if your decision-making ability is impaired. To do this, you can use a document called a **healthcare proxy** (also called a **durable power of attorney for health**).

If you have strong feelings about how you want to be cared for if you're critically ill and can't speak for yourself, then you should think about drafting a **living will**. This is a document that sets forth your feelings about the use of heroic or artificial measures to keep you alive in an end-of-life situation.

Another document commonly used is called a do-not-resuscitate directive (**DNR directive**), which states you do not want to be revived if you are in an end-of-life situation—for example, if you are on a life-support system.

If you don't have a living will or a healthcare proxy or a DNR directive, physicians will consult family members about treatment options. It's important to have these documents in place if you prefer that your life not be extended with heroic measures. It's especially important if the person you would like to be responsible for your health is not a relative, as hospitals rarely give non-relatives the authority to make decisions about treatment.

ASK THE EXPERTS

My elderly father has just been admitted to the hospital, and there's a chance he will need to be put on life-support equipment. He never wrote a living will or healthcare directive—is this a good time to discuss the idea with him?

As long as he is still mentally alert, you can discuss it with him and whatever decision he makes will be honored. However if his illness has affected his judgment or mental capacity, then it's too late because anything he signs at this point probably wouldn't be considered valid.

If I write a living will or healthcare directive, how can I make sure someone will find it when necessary?

Keep it in a place where it could easily be found (e.g., the top drawer of your desk or a clearly marked folder in a filing cabinet). You should also give a copy to the person you name as an agent and one to your family physician.

Dying without a will?

Every state has laws governing how property is inherited if a person dies without a will. These are called **intestacy laws**. If you're married, your spouse and children (if any) are the first to inherit. Then the next heirs would be your parents, then your siblings, and finally your siblings' off-spring. If your estate has any assets, then the probate court (see page 158) will need to appoint someone to administer the process of distributing the estate to your heirs. Because the laws of intestacy follow rigid rules about who inherits property, if you want to leave assets to a particular person (either in or out of the family chain), then having a will is especially important!

now what do I do?

I made a will years ago but many things have changed since then. Can I change it?

You can certainly write a new will, but a **codicil** (a formal amendment to a will) can also provide for the changes. One advantage to drawing up a new will is that there will be no evidence of what you had previously written, since the first version will be destroyed. On the other hand, if you add a codicil to your will, when your will is made public, your heirs will know both what you had originally intended and how you modified it. Keep in mind that it may take as long for your lawyer to do a codicil as it would to prepare a new will.

I have strong feelings about my relatives and want to provide for some and leave out others. Can I divide my estate in whatever way I choose, even if it doesn't look "fair?"

You can do whatever you want in your will, and if you want to make sure that your assets are distributed in the way you want (with limited exceptions), a will is the only way to make those wishes known. One exception, for example, is that you can't completely disinherit a spouse or minor children.

What if I inherit property—does that property automatically go to my spouse as well? Or is it mine to keep if we one day get divorced?

That depends on whether it is kept separately (for example, in a bank account in your name only) or treated like common property (such as real estate with both of your names on the deed). If the former, it will generally be seen as yours rather than shared by the marriage. If the latter, it will generally be considered joint property.

My husband died, and everything we own was in his name. If I don't have the money to hire a lawyer, how can I get it all transferred to me?

Don't be discouraged from talking to a lawyer just because you don't have access to money, especially if you believe you'll have money to pay for a lawyer once the assets are transferred to you. A lawyer may be willing to represent you if you agree that the lawyer's fee will come out of the proceeds of the estate.

My elderly mother is giving away all her money. Can I get power of attorney to manage her affairs?

That's tricky. If she is lucid enough and amenable to naming an attorney-in-fact, she can grant a power of attorney to you or another person of her choosing so that someone can manage her affairs when she is unable to. If she's not of sound mind, a guardianship may also become necessary, but that is a separate decision and one that will involve petitioning the court to show that she's mentally incapable. If the court agrees that she is, it will appoint a guardian to manage her affairs, usually in this order of priority: (1) spouse, (2) adult children, (3) parents, (4) adult siblings.

now where do I go?!

CONTACTS

www.findlaw.com—in the "Public" section, look at "Wills & Trusts" (under "Money") and "Aging and Health."

www.freeadvice.com—offers an extensive question and answer section under these two categories: "Money" and "Aging and Health."

www.nolo.com—"Wills & Estates" section offers a legal encyclopedia, frequently asked questions, and updates.

www.partnershipforcaring.org—contains information related to end-of-life issues including downloadable forms for durable powers of attorney, living wills, and other state-specific documents.

www.growthhouse.org—useful source of information pertaining to end-of-life issues.

BOOKS

The American Bar Association Guide to Wills and Estates

Plan Your Estate
by Denis Clifford & Cora Jordan

Going into Business

what is business law?

You've got a brilliant idea for a new business. Terrific! Better yet, you've figured out how to turn it into an income-generating enterprise—you've even written a business plan. Good for you. But now you're beginning to realize that there are some business law issues to consider, such as whether to set up your business as a corporation or some other legal entity, whether the name you've chosen has already been taken by someone else, how to raise money to finance the business, what laws or regulations govern the industry you're entering, and how to hire employees.

Don't go it alone. You need a business lawyer. Though it's best to get one on board as soon as you've completed your business plan, you can hire a lawyer at any time during your start-up. And once your business is up and running, business lawyers can handle any business negotiations you may have. While you hope that it's all smooth sailing, if you get into any problems along the way, your business lawyer can represent you (or find someone to represent you) in a lawsuit.

Writing a business plan

A **business plan** is a written proposal for your business outlining the basic idea of the business as well as many of the details of how it will operate. A good business plan will also include financial projections for one to five years. Most banks require a detailed business plan before they will lend money to a new business venture. For assistance in preparing a business plan, consult the Web site of the Small Business Administration (**www.sbaonline.sba.gov/starting/indexbusplans.html**).

Questions to ask a business lawyer

When hiring a business lawyer, ask for recommendations from family and friends already in business, as well as people you know through clubs or organizations. If you have an accountant, banker, or insurance broker, ask them. And once you meet with prospective lawyers, ask for client references. People in business talk to their lawyers frequently, so think about whether each lawyer you interview is someone you wouldn't mind spending several hours with, possibly over a meal, while you work out critical issues facing your business. Here are some questions you may want to ask at an initial interview:

How many years of experience do you have? Do you have experience in setting up businesses in all the various legal structures (sole proprietorship, limited liability company, partnership, corporation)?

Have you ever been in business yourself?

How do you charge for your services? Is it by the hour, by the transaction, or some combination?
Note: If your lawyer is a stickler about hourly billing, the clock will be on every time you and she have even a quick phone call.

Do you provide any special assistance to entrepreneurs who are just getting started?
If you have a strong business plan, ask if you can defer paying legal fees until your business gets off the ground.

Would you be able to help me work with banks to obtain funding?

Do you have any knowledge of the particular industry my business is in?
Although it's not essential that your lawyer have experience in your industry, it can be an added bonus.

As my business grows and I hire more personnel, will you be able to handle hiring and firing issues or refer me to an employment-law specialist?

How accessible do you make yourself to your clients? (Can I expect to have my calls returned within 24 hours? Do you take emergency phone calls after business hours?)

sole proprietorship

Going into business for yourself

When you start a business, you need to give it a legal framework. Your choice of structure will affect many things, including how you pay your taxes, your liability in the event of a lawsuit, and how profits (or losses!) are allocated among the owners, if you have one or more partners. There are many different legal structures to choose from.

One of the easiest ways to get started is creating a **sole proprietorship**, where you're in business by yourself. It's the simplest and least expensive way to set up a business (especially if you have no employees) because there is very little legal distinction between you and your business. This transparency is what distinguishes a sole proprietorship, but it also presents some risk. While you may be able to get insurance to cover yourself, you need to understand that if your business is a sole proprietorship, you're potentially exposing all of your assets (even those not connected to your business) to judgments or other debts incurred by the business. So if you're sued, it is not just your business that's on the hook—you are, too!

As your business grows, it may be wise to consider changing its structure to something like an LLC (see page 177) or a corporation (see page 176), both of which provide more insulation from potential liabilities.

For tax purposes, a sole proprietorship is considered the same entity as the individual owner, so you pay the taxes incurred by your business. All this means is that when you pay your federal taxes, your business income will be listed on your individual tax return, with a reference to a special form (usually Schedule C) that records the profits and losses from your business.

ASK THE EXPERTS

Is there anything I need to know about choosing a name for my business?

You need to make sure that the name is not already being used by anyone else who can claim they had "first rights" to it. Once you have a name and have decided what legal structure you're using, your lawyer can check that the name is not being used by another business in your state. If it is, you may have to modify the name a bit so that it's unique. (See also trademarks on page 182 for more information.) There is also the formality of registering your business's name with your state. If you're operating the business under a name other than your legal name, you will need to file what's called a certificate of assumed name to identify that you are "**doing business as**" the name you have chosen (also called a d/b/a).

FIRST PERSON   DISASTER STORY

Tangled up in the same name

I was so excited when I opened my own beauty salon. I named it Hair by Heloise, after my great aunt who had gorgeous red hair. What I didn't know was that just two towns away, a pet groomer was using the exact same name. In my second week of business I got a letter from this other Heloise, charging trademark infringement. I thought the whole thing was so ridiculous that I was sure the judge would throw the case out. Boy, was I wrong. The case wasn't about the rights of two different businesses to have the same name, it was about the likelihood the same name and the geographic proximity would cause confusion for customers. Unfortunately, the judge thought that there was a degree of confusion and ordered me to cease using the name. I wish I had checked with a lawyer about a name search before I went into business. —Sandra K.

partnerships

Sharing the ups and downs

Partnerships are similar to sole proprietorships except that this legal structure lets you have more than one owner. Like sole proprietorships, the business's profits and losses are shared on each partner's individual tax return. Similarly, partners are personally liable for debts and any judgments against their business. Because of this shared liability, it's important to choose your partners wisely!

It's also vital to have a **partnership agreement** that spells out the responsibilities and expectations of the partners. A standard agreement, typically written by a lawyer, will cover many core issues including (1) who contributed what assets to the business, (2) how decisions are to be made, (3) how profits (and losses) are to be allocated, and (4) how the partnership can be dissolved.

Paying taxes for your business

The Internal Revenue Service (IRS) offers many publications to help you understand your tax obligations. Two particularly helpful ones are "Tax Guide for Small Businesses" (publication #334) and "Starting a Business and Keeping Records" (publication #583). You can get copies of these guides at the IRS Web site, **www.irs.gov**.

My business partner has become difficult to work with. How can I get out of the partnership?

When your lawyer drafts your partnership agreement, one of the important sections will cover how to end the partnership. Typically, partnership agreements outline procedures for terminating the relationship for various reasons, ranging from the wrongdoing of a partner to an amicable mutual dissolution. The agreement should also clearly state how the assets of the company should be divided if the partnership ends.

Do all partners have to be equal?

No. Partnerships are structured in many different ways, depending on the agreement between the parties—and often, what each brings to the business. One of the details your partnership agreement should cover is what percentage of the business each partner owns and who controls the various aspects of the business.

Should I hire a business lawyer to review the partnership arrangement my partner's lawyer drew up?

It's a good idea for each partner to consult her own attorney until the partnership is formed. After that, it would be appropriate to have one lawyer represent the partnership.

corporations

How to limit liability

In a **corporation**, the business entity is separate from the people who own it. This gives the owners **limited liability**. That means the individual shareholders of the company won't be personally liable for the debts of the business unless they specifically choose to be (e.g., by personally guaranteeing a business loan). In most instances financial losses or judgments against the corporation are limited to the assets owned by the corporation.

Forming a corporation requires a bit more work and expense than the other legal structures. For example, you need to open a corporate bank account, file a certificate of incorporation with the state, develop **bylaws** (which are rules that govern the corporation), issue stock certificates, and maintain minutes of corporate meetings. These are all things your lawyer will be able to help you with.

Because the corporation is considered a separate entity, it is taxed as such. This means the income the corporation makes is taxed, and any income (also known as **dividends**) that is shared with its individual owners—also called **shareholders**—is also taxed. There are other types of corporations as well, and tax implications will vary based on the type of corporation involved.

ASK THE EXPERTS

How do I know which business structure is right for my business?

That depends on many factors, but the most important one is your financial liability. For example, if you own a business that exposes you to liabilities that are greater than your assets and insurance could cover (e.g., you own a fleet of taxis), you might want to form a corporation or LLC to limit your financial liability to the amount you have invested in your business. Another factor is size. Many businesses begin as a sole proprietorship when they have small debts, few employees, and a simple business plan. But then as the business grows, it changes and becomes a partnership or corporation.

Won't business insurance cover me from all liabilities?

While having adequate insurance coverage should protect you from anticipated risks, there are some risks you can't plan for or that aren't covered by your insurance (e.g., judgments in certain legal cases).

If I start a corporation, can I pay my home expenses out of my business account?

No! In order to preserve the legal protection afforded by corporate status, you need to keep a strict separation between yourself and the business. If you're sloppy and draw no distinctions between your money and that of your business, you could expose yourself to liability for your business debts.

What about LLCs?

Another popular way to organize a business is as an LLC, which stands for limited liability company. This is a hybrid structure that offers the limited liability benefits of a corporation but allows you to be taxed like a partnership. In other words, it shields your assets (such as your home) in case you're sued, and it will be taxed only once as in a partnership. An LLC is an attractive way to structure a business because of these twin benefits. To set up an LLC, most states require that you file a document called Articles of Organization. LLCs are not permissible for businesses in certain industries (such as architects or certain health-care providers), so you will need to consult with your lawyer about whether an LLC is a viable structure for your business.

buying a business

Starting a business from scratch isn't the only option if you want to be your own boss—you can also buy an existing business. If you choose this path, there are different legal issues to consider.

For starters, you should never buy a business without doing what's known as **due diligence** (conducting a thorough examination of the business's health and finances). The purpose of due diligence is for the potential buyer to get a better understanding of the nature of the business and its financial situation.

Typically, the owner of the business will cooperate in this process by making his books and records available to a serious buyer (who may first be asked to sign a **confidentiality agreement** to not disclose any information revealed). Depending on the type of business, the process may involve reviewing the business's contracts with suppliers and key employees, financial records (including tax returns, bank statements, etc.), office leases, and any other documents that are critical to the business. It's also a good idea to interview customers and suppliers and inspect any buildings or property involved in the purchase.

Once you decide to purchase a business, you will negotiate the terms of the sale with the owner and ultimately come to terms— which will then be outlined in a sale contract. The contract will cover such issues as how the purchase price is to be paid, who is obligated for what liabilities, and how to deal with **accounts receivable** (money coming in from customers) and **accounts payable** (money owed to creditors). Your lawyer will be able to walk you through all of these details.

I've just bought a business, and now I realize that many customers are severely delinquent in their payments. What can I do?

This is just the kind of surprise you hope to avoid by doing due diligence before the sale. This is why you need to review all the financial statements of a business. If you didn't ask for that kind of information, you're stuck with what you bought and will likely have no recourse. On the other hand, if the seller misrepresented something in the deal (e.g., she gave you a certified statement as to credits and debits but omitted information), you can sue for breach of contract or misrepresentation.

The owner listed "good will" as one of the items I'll be purchasing. What is he talking about?

Good will refers to those qualities of a business that are difficult to put a price on but often are its most valued assets—like its name, its relationships in the business community, or its loyal customer following. It is basically the value of the business over and above the value of its hard assets (like cash and inventory). Thus it's common for contracts to include provisions such as the transfer of customer lists, the retention of the owner as a consultant during a transition period, or other methods of assuring that a business's good will is carried forward.

buying a franchise

Sharing the success

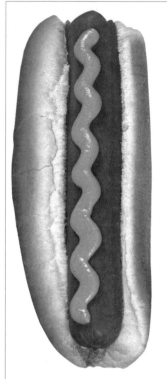

For more information about franchises, visit the Web site of the Federal Trade Commission, the agency that regulates these relationships (**www.ftc.gov/bcp/ menu-fran.htm**).

Another way to get started in business is to buy a franchise. A **franchise** is a license to operate a branch of an existing business with an established brand name, such as McDonald's or Mailboxes Etc. Among other things, the franchise's brand name should ensure a solid customer base. For this reason, buying a franchise is a good option if you want to learn about a business before starting your own from scratch.

To buy a franchise, you'll need to sign a complex contract with the **franchisor** (the company that grants you the license to operate the business). The terms of these agreements can be complicated, so it's a good idea to have the contract reviewed by a lawyer. Also be prepared to have your creditworthiness and your business background thoroughly investigated.

As a **franchisee** (the legal term for a person who operates a franchise), you receive certain benefits, such as access to corporate information, the use of the company's trademarks and other proprietary (confidential) materials. In return, you're required to run the business according to standards outlined by the franchisor—and most important, you agree to pay a fee or distribute a percentage of the revenues or profits to the franchisor.

ASK THE EXPERTS

If I buy a franchise of a restaurant chain, and a customer slips and injures himself there, who defends against a lawsuit—me or the franchisor?

Typically such accidents would be covered by your insurance, not the franchisor's. Your franchise agreement will likely require you to carry a certain amount of insurance to protect against this kind of accident, but the details will vary depending on your agreement.

What happens if I decide to sell the franchise?

That depends on the provisions of your franchise agreement. If you think you may want to sell the franchise one day, look at the section of the agreement that deals with transferring your rights. It may be prohibited or allowed as long as you follow certain procedures and the buyer meets any criteria spelled out in the franchise agreement.

intellectual property

Basic rules about copyrights, trademarks, and patents

Some of the most valuable assets owned by your company are not its cash reserves but something intangible called **intellectual property**—the legal term that covers trademarks, copyrights, and patents, among other things. Should your business involve any of these, it would be wise to consult a lawyer who specializes in intellectual property. In fact, these areas are so specialized that an intellectual-property lawyer may have a specialty within these areas—so don't be surprised if a trademark lawyer doesn't know too much about patent law.

Copyright protects the expression of ideas and artistic work, allowing the creator or owner to control how they are used. Only the legal holder of a right under copyright law can sell or give that right to another. This right is in place for a finite period of time (the length of copyright protection varies, but for works created after 1977, copyright protection lasts for a period equal to the life of the author plus 70 years). Once the time limit is up, the work enters into the **public domain**, a legal state where it can be used for free by anyone. If your business does a lot of advertising or has to do with publishing or the arts, copyright is an area of law you'd like your lawyer to be quite familiar with. For more information, contact the Copyright Society of the U.S.A. at **www.csusa.org**.

When you see an "R" in a circle following a word or phrase, that indicates that the mark is a registered trademark. If you see a "TM," that means the user has not registered the name as a trademark, but is claiming trademark rights on it. A small "c" in a circle is used to designate copyrighted material; however, the lack of this mark does not necessarily mean the material has not been copyrighted.

A **trademark** gives you the exclusive right to use a word, phrase, logo, or other identifier as a brand name. Before claiming an identifier as a trademark, you need to be sure that no one else is using it. A lawyer who specializes in trademark law can search among all the registered and unregistered trademarks to see if anyone else has claimed trademark rights and advise you on claiming and protecting your rights. Then if a competitor uses that name, you can bring suit against them to stop them from using your trademark. While the amount of legal protection will vary, trademark holders have rights even when their marks are not registered. For more information contact the International Trademark Association: **www.inta.org**.

Patents give innovators of original inventions, as well as original methods or processes, legal protection from competition in the market place for a limited amount of time (between 17 and 20 years, depending on when the patent was issued). This allows the inventor to be the first to sell his invention in the market and, for a set amount of time, forbids competitors from copying the invention. After the patent expires, others can enter the market, but the original maker will have had a head start in building a business around the invention. For more information contact the American Intellectual Property Law Association at **www.aipla.org**.

hiring employees

Complying with labor laws

Great, your business is up and running. In fact, you're doing so well that you need to hire people to help you. But before you place that first "help wanted" ad, you need to be aware of certain employment laws, such as regulations governing workplace conditions and laws prohibiting discrimination.

Workplace discrimination laws basically come down to a simple principle: It is illegal to discriminate in employment on the basis of gender, age, religious beliefs, national origin, physical or mental disability, race, or color. (For more on this see page 20.)

It's also important to understand the difference between employees and independent contractors (also called freelancers), because you'll have to treat the two types of workers differently. **Employees** are people who work for you, on either a part-time or full-time basis. You are responsible for providing certain benefits, such as disability insurance and workers' compensation, based on the requirements of your state. You must also withhold a portion of their paycheck for taxes that you forward to the tax authorities. When you set up your payroll (which you can do on your own or through a payroll service), you'll need a system to pay federal and often state and city taxes on behalf of your employees.

Independent contractors (also known as freelancers or consultants) are self-employed service providers. They hire out their time and/or expertise for a fee or on a per-hour basis. If you retain any independent contractors, you don't have to provide benefits for them or withhold their taxes (they're responsible for paying their own taxes). In order to make sure they're not considered employees for tax purposes, you must be careful that they operate as independent contractors (e.g., maintain their own office at their own expense and limit their time at your office).

ASK THE EXPERTS

Can I hire someone who is not a U.S. citizen?

You need to check that foreign-born employees have the proper documentation to legally work in the United States. Ideally, they need to provide you with their Social Security number, a green card, or a certificate of naturalization. Employing illegal aliens can result in fines or even imprisonment for the employer.

What do I have to worry about when firing an employee?

Most employment situations are considered **employment at will**, which means as an employer you can fire your employees as you see fit. But there are limitations. You still cannot fire employees in a discriminatory fashion. And if the employee has a contract with you, you will have to follow the terms of that contract regarding termination. For example, if the employee is entitled to **severance payments** upon termination, you must pay whatever amount the contract stipulates. **Downsizing** (firing groups of people at a time) can create many legal problems, especially if you employ more than 100 people. If your business is this large, make sure to review your layoff plan with a lawyer.

I would like to hire a high school student. Are there any special rules about hiring minors?

Hiring minors is regulated by both state and federal law. Under federal law, you can hire minors for certain types of nonhazardous work as long as you comply with certain guidelines (e.g., the youth cannot work during school hours). To review the provisions of the federal law (the Fair Labor Standards Act), you can visit the Web site of the Department of Labor (**www.dol.gov**). Each state also has its own laws regarding hiring minors, so you will also need to comply with the laws in your state.

Confidentiality agreements

If you feel your business has proprietary information, such as **trade secrets**, that your employees are exposed to, one way to protect yourself is to have your employees sign a noncompete and/or a confidentiality agreement. A **noncompete** agreement means your employees cannot work for a direct competitor for a certain length of time after leaving your employment. A **confidentiality agreement** prevents your employees from disclosing trade secrets acquired during their employment. Keep in mind that only information that is actually confidential and proprietary can be protected. For example, if someone trained as a chef in your catering shop, she can certainly use her cooking skills in another job after she quits. But if she took the company's recipe book, such action would most likely be a violation of the confidentiality agreement.

now what do I do?
Answers to common questions

Do I need to get insurance for my business?

Most businesses should carry **general liability insurance** to protect against injuries on the premises and general business risks. You may also be required by your landlord or your lender to have certain types of insurance (e.g., flood insurance if your business is located in an area with a high flood risk). Talk with your insurance broker about what kind of insurance makes sense for your business. Your state may also require businesses to carry **workers' compensation** insurance (see page 16), which covers employees who get injured during the course of their employment.

I want to run my business out of my home. Are there any restrictions on doing that?

This depends on your town's zoning regulations. Some municipalities restrict types of businesses as well as where businesses can be located. If you're a consultant and your business doesn't create a lot of traffic, noise, or pollution, you shouldn't run into problems. Most local zoning boards are concerned with home businesses that create excess traffic that could pose a burden on neighbors.

What if my business is raising money for a charitable purpose?

If your business fits certain criteria defined by your state, you may be able to qualify for **nonprofit status** (a special legal classification for companies that exist to benefit the public good in some way). Nonprofit corporations have certain tax advantages, such as exemption from income taxes on income related to the nonprofit activities and exemptions from real estate property taxes. Advising nonprofit corporations is a particular legal specialty. Often law firms will offer **pro bono** representation for nonprofit entities (meaning they'll do the legal work for free). Contact your local bar association for recommendations.

Can I mail out a photocopy of a newspaper article that reviewed my restaurant?

No. When a newspaper or magazine publishes an article, it owns the copyright to the article. This means that no one else can reproduce the article without their permission. In order to avoid trouble, contact the newspaper's rights and permissions office and see if you can buy reprints of the article for your mailing.

now where do I go?!

CONTACTS

The U.S. Department of Labor's Small Business Handbook, **www.dol.gov/dol/asp/ public/programs/handbook/main.htm**—offers a guide tailored to small businesses.

Small Business Administration, **www.sbaonline.sba.gov**—site of the federal government's Small Business Administration (SBA). For assistance with problems call 800-827-5722.

www. freeadvice.com—offers an extensive question and answer section under the "Business Law" heading, as well as live chats with lawyers.

BOOKS

How to Write a Business Plan
by Mike McKeever

The Legal Guide for Starting and Running a Small Business, Volume 1
by Fred S. Steingold

Free Agent Nation
by Daniel Pink

meet our experts

Jane Altman, the founding and managing partner in the law firm, Altman & Legband in Princeton, New Jersey, has been practicing law for 24 years. As a matrimonial and family law specialist, she counsels individuals on a variety of domestic matters including prenuptial agreements, separation and divorce, and domestic violence. She contributed to the Family Law chapter.
She can be reached at **jradpl@aol.com.**

Amy Blumenthal, who has practiced law for 9 years, is a partner in the law firm of Blumenthal and Gruber, LLP, in Dallas, Texas. She is a trial lawyer specializing in representing plaintiffs in product liability and catastrophic-injury cases. Amy contributed to the Personal-Injury Law chapter and the car accident section of the Your Car chapter.
She can be reached at **amblumenthal@aol.com.**

Michael Brennan, a general practitioner in Framingham, Massachusetts, specializes in the defense of criminal cases. In addition, he represents individuals in probate and family court, and advises small businesses on a variety of matters. Before founding his own practice in 1997, he served as an assistant district attorney for seven years, prosecuting serious felony cases in Middlesex County, Massachusetts. Michael contributed to the Run-ins with the Law chapter and the drunk driving, speeding, and traffic court sections of the Your Car chapter.
He can be reached at **mdbrennan@rcn.com.**

Irwin Dinn, a founding member of the Cleveland law firm, Dinn, Hochman, Potter & Levy, has over 35 years of experience in assisting individuals in the areas of estate planning, taxation, and family business succession. He also specializes in issues relating to long-term illnesses, disability, and aging. He contributed to the Wills and Trusts chapter. He can be reached at **idinn@dhplaw.com**.

Carla J. Feldman, who has been practicing law for 17 years, is a partner with the Los Angeles office of the law firm, Loeb & Loeb, LLP. Her practice focuses on litigating cases on a wide variety of workplace matters, including wrongful termination, discrimination, sexual harassment, and workplace violence. She also counsels clients on negotiating employment contracts, severance, and other job-related matters. She contributed to the On the Job and Going into Business chapters. She can be reached at **cfeldman@loeb.com**.

Richard Feuerstein is a partner in the law firm of Feuerstein & Murphy in San Diego. He has been a certified specialist in family law since 1991. He contributed to the Family Law chapter. He can be reached at **rich@rpflaw.com**.

Helene Godin is a partner in the New York City law firm Wolff & Godin. She specializes in intellectual property law, with an emphasis on publishing, entertainment and media law issues. Her clients include publishing and other media corporations, as well as numerous artists, authors and illustrators.

She can be reached at **hgodin@wolffgodin.com**.

Brad Jackson has been practicing law in Dallas since 1990. He is a trial lawyer who represents plaintiffs in personal injury and commercial litigation matters. He contributed to the Personal-Injury Law chapter and the car accident section of the Your Car chapter.

He can be reached at **brad@airmail.net**.

Craig Thor Kimmel is a partner in the law firm of Kimmel & Silverman, which has offices in New Jersey and Pennsylvania. He specializes in representing consumers in cases involving warranty problems. He has practiced law for 12 years. He contributed to the lemon law section of the Your Car chapter.

He can be reached at **ckimmel@lemonlaw.com**.

Richard Klein is a solo practitioner in New York City with 13 years of experience. He specializes in commercial and residential real estate law as well as general business matters. In addition to his law practice, he is a restaurateur, something that gives him first-hand experience in many of the legal matters he handles for his clients. He contributed to both the Home and Going into Business chapters.
He can be reached at **www.richkleinlaw@aol.com**.

Douglas M. Neistat, who has been practicing law for over 29 years, is a partner with the law firm Greenberg & Bass in Encino, California. An active member of the American Bankruptcy Institute and the Los Angeles Bankruptcy Forum, he represents both individual and corporate clients in all aspects of debt management and bankruptcy. He is a frequent lecturer on bankruptcy-related topics. He contributed to the Money and Credit chapter.
He can be reached at **dneistat@greenbass.com**.

Lynne Strober heads the family law department of the West Orange, New Jersey law firm Mandelbaum, Salsburg, Gold, Lazris, Discenza & Steinberg. Her practice involves all areas of divorce litigation. She and her law partner, Craig Alexander, contributed to the adoption section of the Family Law chapter.
She can be reached at **lstrober@mandelbaumsalsburg.com**.

glossary

Acquittal   A decision by a judge or jury that finds the defendant not guilty.

Affidavit   A signed statement made under oath or in the presence of a court officer or representative.

Alimony   After a divorce, money paid by one ex-spouse to the other. The amount and duration of payments are determined by the court or in a settlement.

Annulment   A court procedure that voids a marriage, making it as if the marriage was never legally performed.

Arbitration   A method of resolving disputes using a neutral third party other than a judge and/or jury. Often faster and less costly than formal court proceedings, arbitration can still be legally binding.

Arraignment   A court appearance in which a defendant is formally presented with charges against her and is given the opportunity to plead (that is, to admit to or deny the charges).

Beneficiary   A person or organization entitled to receive money or other assets through a will, trust, or insurance policy.

Breach   Failure to fulfill a legal obligation; often used to describe failure to meet the terms of a contract.

Burden of Proof   The responsibility of satisfying a judge or jury that a certain version of the facts is true. In a civil trial, the plaintiff must demonstrate that "a preponderance of evidence"—over 50%—is in his or her favor.

In a criminal trial, there's a higher bar, and the government must show beyond a reasonable doubt that the defendant is guilty.

Cause of Action   The legal basis, such as negligence or breach of contract, used to bring a lawsuit.

Civil Law   These cases generally involve private property rights and remedies (e.g., real estate, divorce), as opposed to criminal cases, which involve violations of laws pertaining to illegal conduct. (See Criminal Law.)

Class Action   A case in which many people who have been similarly injured or have used the same defective product join together to sue a person or organization (often a company).

Codicil   An amendment to a will that can clarify, add to, or otherwise modify the original document. Like a will, it must be signed in front of witnesses.

Common Law Marriage   In states where it is recognized, a couple who cohabitate for a certain number of years and intend to marry are treated as if they were legally married.

Community Property   Property acquired during a marriage. In states where community property is recognized, such property belongs equally to each party regardless of who made the effort to acquire it.

Compensatory Damages   Monetary awards that cover injury or financial loss.

Contingency Fee   Rather than an hourly fee, an arrangement in which a lawyer only gets paid if she wins the case (the fee comes out of the money awarded in the case). This is common practice with personal-injury lawyers.

Contract   A legally binding agreement involving two or more people or businesses that describes what the participants will or will not do. Contracts can be written or oral, but some agreements require documentation to be legally enforceable.

Copyright   The right to make, copy, perform, sell, market, or publish an artistic work or expression of an idea.

Covenant   In real estate, a limitation that determines use; for instance, the requirement that a piece of land be used solely for agricultural purposes. Though most common in real estate, covenants—written promises or agreements—exist in other legal contexts as well.

Criminal Law   Criminal laws make specific behaviors illegal, and in order to be found guilty, a defendant must be proven to have acted with intent. Criminal laws are punishable by fines and/or imprisonment, as well as other measures. (See Civil Law.)

Deed   A document that transfers legal ownership of property.

Defendant   A person or organization accused of committing wrongdoing in a civil or criminal case. In a civil case, a plaintiff brings a lawsuit against a defendant. In a criminal case, the government brings the lawsuit or charges. (See Plaintiff.)

Deposition   A pretrial process in which one party questions another or a witness. During a deposition, all questions must be answered under oath and recorded by a court reporter. The transcript or videotape of a deposition can be entered as testimony in a trial.

Discovery   A court-governed investigation that is conducted before trial. Through discovery, parties can question each other and sometimes witnesses, and can compel each other to provide documents or physical evidence.

Do-Not-Resuscitate Directive   Commonly referred to by its initials, DNR, a document that states that a person does not want to be revived in an end-of-life situation, such as being on a life-support system.

Due Diligence   In a business transaction, the process of conducting a thorough examination of a business entity.

Employment at Will   An employer's right to fire an employee at any time.

Equitable Distribution   In divorce, a standard, followed in many states, for fairly dividing property acquired during the marriage.

Escrow   A document, asset, or sum of money held by a neutral third party that is turned over to the owner or grantee after a specified condition is met.

Ex Parte   A legal proceeding in which only one party is present, generally because the other party was not given notice.

Evidence   Information presented to a judge or jury to convince them of the truthfulness of facts presented in a trial. Documents, photographs, testimony of witnesses, and laboratory reports are common types of evidence.

Executor   The person named in a will who is appointed to manage the property of the deceased.

Healthcare Proxy   A person authorized to make choices about medical treatment for another person—called the principal—if the principal's decision-making ability is impaired.

Hearsay   Secondhand testimony, which in many circumstances is disallowed as evidence in a trial.

Litigation   The process of using the courts to resolve a legal dispute.

Living Will   A signed document that sets forth a person's desires about what kind of medical treatment he or she would like to receive and whether artificial means should be used to prolong life. The document takes effect if the person becomes unable to communicate his or her wishes.

Limited Liability Company   A business structure that shields the assets of the owners and also allows a company the benefits of being taxed like a partnership. Commonly referred to by its initials, LLC.

Mediation   An alternative to litigation, in which a neutral third party facilitates communication and a mutually acceptable agreement between parties involved in a conflict.

The mediator does not determine or impose the outcome, which is called a settlement. (See Settlement.)

Negligence   A legal standard in which a person can be held responsible for harm she has caused unintentionally if it can be shown that the individual failed to act as a reasonable person would have in similar circumstances.

No-fault Divorce   Allows the parties to end a marriage without assigning fault—such as infidelity—to either spouse. In no-fault divorce, one party can claim that the marriage is no longer working, for such reasons as irreconcilable differences, incompatibility, or an irretrievable breakdown of the relationship.

Palimony   After an unmarried couple splits up, a term used to describe alimony-like support given by one party to another.

Partnership   A business structure in which two or more people own a business together; usually, each partner contributes money, property, or labor in exchange for a share of the business. The partners can share proportionately in the profits and losses of the venture.

Patent   An exclusive right, often referred to as a limited monopoly, granted to an inventor (either a company or an individual) to make, use, or sell an invention for a set number of years.

Plaintiff   A person, corporation, or other legal entity that brings a lawsuit; those who sue another party. The defendant, or defendants, are those accused. (See Defendant.)

Power of Attorney A document that gives one person the authority to make legal decisions for another.

Probate A court process that ratifies a will and allows an executor to fulfill the terms of the will.

Pro se A defendant who represents herself in court.

Punitive Damages Awards that go beyond compensatory damages and are intended to punish a losing party's malevolent actions.

Rider An addition to a contract or lease, covering a unique arrangement between the parties.

Settlement An agreement, reached between parties in a conflict, that reduces or resolves differences.

Statute of Limitations The time frame in which a lawsuit must be filed, following an injury or breach of contract.

Strict Liability In tort cases, a standard that holds a defendant liable—regardless of intent, negligence, or fault—as long as it can be proven that the defendant's action caused the damage.

Subpoena A court order that requires a person to be present at a certain time and place—usually to serve as a witness in a trial—or face a penalty.

Tender Years Presumption In a divorce, a doctrine that holds that if the mother and father are equally good parents, the children—particularly those under the age of six—are most likely better off with the mother.

Testator A person who makes a valid will.

Title Evidence of ownership of property.

Tort The body of law that holds legally responsible a person who caused injury to another. A tort can be intentional but is usually not.

Trademark The exclusive right to use a brand name.

Trade Secret Generally, a formula, device, or idea that gives a company a competitive advantage and is handled in a manner intended to prevent the public or competitors from learning about it.

Treble Damages Legal term to describe the tripling of monetary damages in a case. Treble damages are awarded in certain types of cases, often because a statute provides for them as a punitive measure.

Trust A legal entity created to hold assets on behalf of a benefiting party.

Verdict The final decision of a jury in a trial.

Voir Dire At the outset of a trial, the process of questioning prospective jurors and selecting a panel. Also, during a trial, a side hearing held to determine the admissibility of certain evidence; during this procedure, the jury is excused.

Waiver The act of intentionally renouncing a right or claim.

index

the author: up close

Marci Alboher Nusbaum is a lawyer and freelance journalist who writes about the law, workplace issues, and travel. She holds an undergraduate degree in English from the University of Pennsylvania and a law degree from American University's Washington College of Law. She practiced law for 8 years, first at a law firm and then in various corporate settings. She is a frequent speaker about career issues for lawyers and also teaches a writing class for lawyers and other professionals. Her work has appeared in numerous publications including *The New York Times, Time Out New York, Travel and Leisure, The National Law Journal, The New York Law Journal,* and *New York Lawyer.* She can be reached at **heymarci@hotmail.com.** She lives in Manhattan with her husband, Gary.

Barbara J. Morgan Publisher, Silver Lining Books

I think I need a Lawyer, Now What?! ™

Barb Chintz Editorial Director

Leonard Vigliarolo Design Director

Susan Stellin Editor

Ann Stewart Picture Research

Emily Seese Editorial Assistant

Della R. Mancuso Production Manager

Picture Credits

Artville: 3, 5 *bottom,* 12, 18, 22, 24, 30, 33, 38, 44, 47, 56, 60, 66, 68, 79, 89, 96, 125, 135 *background,* 136, 140, 148, 160, 170, 174, 178; **Comstock:** 135 *inset;* **Corbis:** 4 *top,* 14, 50, 55 *inset,* 111 *inset,* 112, 116, 128; **Digital Stock:** 153 *inset,* 180; **Eyewire:** 58; **Getty Images:** 1, 4 *bottom,* 29 *background,* 46, 95, 98, 102, 114, 156; **PhotoDisc:** 5 *top,* 7 *inset,* 29 *inset,* 36, 70, 77, 78, 80, 84, 111 *background,* 118, 126, 146, 162, 164, 169, 176, 184; **RubberBall Productions:** 72